# JAPANESE KARATE

## A Warrior's Spirit

by Dan Ivan
and
Paul Godshaw

JAPANESE KARATE A Warrior's Spirit
by Dan Ivan and Paul Godshaw

Copyright © 2025 I&I SPORTS SUPPLY. All rights reserved. Published by I&I SPORTS SUPPLY ISBN 978-0-934489-92-8

# Contents

Author's Profiles .................................................................................. vii

Foreword ............................................................................................. xi

History of Japanese Karate ............................................................... xiii

Introduction ........................................................................................ xv

Chapters

1. Body Weapons and Targets ............................................................ 1
2. Stances and Footwork .................................................................. 43
3. Blocks and Evasion ...................................................................... 53
4. Self-Defense Techniques ............................................................. 63
5. Throws and Sweeps ..................................................................... 91
6. Defenses Against Grabs and Holds ........................................... 103
7. Chokes and Submission Holds .................................................. 117
8. Ground Fighting ......................................................................... 129
9. Proper Falls to Prevent Injuries ................................................. 137
10. Stretches and Exercises for Mobility, Strength and Health ...... 145
11. First Strike Concepts .................................................................. 157
12. Key Points and Strategies .......................................................... 165
13. Basic Terminology ..................................................................... 169

# Author's Profile: Dan Ivan

Dan Ivan *sensei* entered the U.S. Army in 1945 at age 15 and learned unarmed combat during basic training. This piqued his interest so much that in 1948, when he arrived in Japan, he began seriously studying the martial arts.

Ivan started judo training at the Kodokan Judo Institute and also took *skotokan* karate with Isao Obata sensei, a true master and legend of his time.

Having Obata sensei as his original instructor was the most significant and important part of Ivan's martial arts career. Obata sensei was the finest role model a newcomer could ask for. He was a leader, a humble gentleman of great stature and he had lots of integrity. He made students understand the importance of spirit, respect and honor. As one of grandmaster Gichin Funakoshi's first disciples, Obata sensei was also recognized for having powerful, outstanding techniques.

At the Kodokan, Shizuya Sato, a young sensei, befriended Ivan and introduced him to many different arts and their leaders. This launched Ivan on a lifelong pursuit of martial arts that earned him black belts in karate, judo, *aikido* and *kendo*. Today, Sato sensei is chief director of the prestigious International Martial Arts Federation World headquarters in Tokyo.

In those early years, when the Japan Karate Association (JKA) was formed, Obata sensei was a part of this group, so Ivan continued training there with Nakayama, Kase and other sensei of that time. Most notable was Kenji Yamamoto, a JKA senior from Hosei University, whose amazing kicks, *kata* and technique added so much to Ivan's education.

Yamamoto sensei then became instructor to the Criminal Investigation Unit Ivan was assigned to at the time. Obata, Yamamoto and other notable masters soon became disappointed with the direction the JKA was going, so they withdrew their support. In 1963, on one of his trips to Japan, Ivan also resigned from the JKA.

Ivan sensei considers his foundation shotokan karate, but he also briefly learned *goju-ryu, shito-ryu* and *wado-ryu* from the top leaders of those systems. He finds merit in all arts from China, Japan, Okinawa, the Philippines, Indonesia and Korea. Ivan points out that it is the instructor — more than the art — that is paramount to learning.

Two prominent sensei that Ivan sponsored to America are Fumio Demura (shito-ryu) and Kiyoshi Yamazaki (shotokan). Both of these leaders follow the concepts and principles of budo.

Now in his 70s, Ivan is retired and gives an occasional clinic or seminar to stress the importance of building good character by teaching students respect and manners. The martial arts, especially in this chaotic world, definitely help build a person's character, providing the instructor himself understands this essential fact.

Ivan heartily endorses Paul Godshaw sensei, a man of integrity and co-author of this book, for teaching the true spirit and traditions of the martial arts. Looking back on his life, Ivan sensei feels blessed to have lived and trained in an era of so many great men and women of the martial arts.

# Author's Profile: Paul Godshaw

Paul Godshaw sensei began training in shotokan karate with Dan Ivan in 1965. When Fumio Demura arrived in America with Ivan, Godshaw added *shito-ryu* karate and *kobudo* to his training.

Since that time, Godshaw has visited Japan frequently and was privileged to train with other notable sensei, such as Hirokazu Kanazawa of shotokan, Hironori Ohtsuka of *wado-ryu*, Gogen Yamaguchi of goju-ryu and Ryusho Sakagami of itosu-kai.

For his extensive background in the martial arts, Godshaw sensei was appointed National Director for the prestigious world headquarters of the International Martial Arts Federation in Japan.

It has always been Ivan's sensei policy to train his black belts in other martial arts, so Godshaw sensei continued training in Yoshinkan Aikido with master Gozo Shioda, *jujutsu* with master Minoru Mochizuki, *judo* and *nihon jujitsu* with 1MAF director Sato sensei, and other arts.

After many years of training, Godshaw sensei became a full-time karate instructor. His headquarters are in Mission Viejo, California. Recognized for his versatility and leadership in the martial arts, Godshaw was appointed as liaison for the World Karate Championships in 1975. Currently, Godshaw sensei is the regional director for the USA AAU Program and chief referee for the AAU Karate Program of America.

The International Martial Arts Federation and the Japan Karate Federation of America have both awarded Godshaw sensei the designation of shihan so that today, he offers his guidance and instruction to all who are sincere in learning.

# Foreword

## Dan Ivan and the Warrior Spirit

by Jose Fraguas

My admiration for Dan Ivan stems from my boyhood fascination with the masters of martial arts. From well-worn books and magazines picked up hot off the press, I learned about the great martial artists.

Meanwhile, my friends were following the escapades of Captain Marvel, Batman and Superman. Sure, my heroes had their frailties, but they were real flesh and blood, not just imaginary creations of paper and ink. Being only 10 years old, I fantasized that one day I would grow up and be lucky enough to become friends with these martial art giants. Thus, when I came to America and met Dan Ivan, it was literally a dream come true.

Dan Ivan stands out as a glamorous and significant figure in American martial arts. An elegant and well-mannered man in a violent art, he brought the fighting style of an obscure island named "Okinawa" to the West. He did this by personal dedication, perseverance and force of will. By personally choosing a few good men to spread the word with him, he became responsible for the attention the American masses paid to Japanese martial arts.

But Dan Ivan is far more than "just" a karate teacher. He was a criminal investigator with the U.S. military occupation force in Japan after WW II. Ivan was also one of the first Westerners to forget the hatred of the war and start building bridges. He did this by studying karate with his former enemies. Ignoring the harsh words of Eastern and Western critics who questioned his openness, Ivan's strength of character and strong personal morals enabled him to forge friendships with many of the top martial arts masters of shattered post-war Japan. And these last until this day.

An example of understanding, patience and tolerance, Ivan is also humble, charming and knowledgeable. He is a true icon of American karate. Moreover, he has trained with such notables as Isao Obata, Gogen Yamaguchi, Gozo Shioda, and Ryusho Sakagami —just to name a few. This makes practitioners around the world, who would give up their first born for 10 percent of this man's experiences, look at him with respect and envy.

I have been in the martial arts for almost three decades now and have encountered thousands of practitioners and teachers. Among all those, I can count on one hand the number of true masters and leaders I have met.

The true warrior spirit, the attitude and etiquette that I admired in the heroes of my youth, is uncommon today, not understood and often misinterpreted. Dan Ivan epitomizes the traditional values that the warrior arts represent. A half-century of budo experience is contained within this Old World gentleman. Now in his 70s, he's still fit and vital, with a sharp, inquiring mind. Ivan shares his experience and knowledge to the martial arts world with "*Japanese Karate: The Warrior Spirit.*"

A Spanish proverb says, "Talking about bulls is not the same as being in the bullring."

In the same manner, it takes a true warrior to talk about the warrior spirit. Dan Ivan is one of those special men who have truly been "in the bullring."

# History of Japanese Karate

American servicemen returning from Japan in the 1940s first introduced us to karate as we know it today. Prior to that, in the 1920s and 1930s, there were Japanese and Okinawans living in Hawaii who were teaching the art on a limited scale.

Versions of this hand-to-hand fighting art prevailed throughout the Asian countries. Japan, China, Korea, the Philippines, Indonesia and others all had similar arts under different names.

Japan credits Gichin Funakoshi, a scholar and martial artist from Okinawa, for introducing karate to them. The year was about 1922. Okinawa had an orderly and systematic way of teaching the art, and this is basically what is now known throughout the world.

The Okinawans, in turn, attribute much of their version of the art to China, which was a major influence on the Ryuku Islands long before the Japanese occupation in the 16th century.

However, in their constant struggle to defend their tiny island nation, the Japanese developed many systems of fighting, including striking and kicking techniques. This occurred long before Funakoshi introduced karate through the ministry of education. It's a fascinating piece of history to note that Japan, so small in size and population compared to her neighbor countries, never lost a war until she lost to America and the allied forces.

It is not accolades we wish to bestow upon Japan for her tenacity in fighting, but we must recognize her indomitable spirit. It takes constant practice and hard training to acquire a fighting skill, and the proper mental attitude is paramount. That spirit is necessary to make it all come together.

The American servicemen who learned this art in the early days of the occupation of Japan returned home to establish roots that still exist today. Karate has diversified in what is taught, what is emphasized and how it is taught. Times today are different and adjustments must be made to accommodate new lifestyles and philosophies.

Today, Japanese karate is still recognized as a martial art for combat, but students are also improving their health through its agile coordination exercises. Regardless of which path you take or teach, your underlying principle should be to improve your well-being and confidence. It is especially important to develop a strong mind, a warrior spirit.

# Introduction

It was the fortunate experience of the authors to train in the Japanese style of karate. Had we trained in one of the arts from China, Okinawa, Korea or any other country, then this text would have been different. To be sure, there is great merit to all arts of various origins. However, we will present Japanese karate and the spirit that is so deeply embodied in all martial arts that come from Japan.

There are many textbooks and training videos on this subject, covering basic kata, sport, free sparring and other elements of this art. Even we have written some of this, so there is no need to repeat that which today is fairly common knowledge.

Rather, we will attempt to present karate in its original concept, a martial art born from the need to survive. Survival from invaders, survival on the battlefield, and in most instances, survival in life-and-death struggles.

## In the Beginning

Japanese karate — and its related arts of judo, jujutsu, aikido, kendo and *iaido* — were conceived and refined on battlefields in warfare.

With the demise of the shogun, warlords and the samurai era, these arts and their tradition evolved into an art, then in some aspect a sport, a way to practice without killing or disabling each other during practice.

Here we are today, in the 21st century, with an estimated five million karate practitioners in the United States alone. Throughout the years, another 50 million or so have studied the art since it arrived here nearly 60 years ago.

The reason for this tremendous surge in popularity can be attributed to its character-building aspects. Many compare learning karate to joining the military. You learn discipline, respect, courtesy, and manners, and begin to build your body and mind. These are all-important aspects of budo and the spirit of Japanese karate.

Modifying this dangerous art to a sport has also made room for our children to participate. They too can enjoy all of the benefits that will help build them into better and stronger citizens of virtue as they grow. Women, of course, are included and practice along side men, developing the very same skills.

## Origins and Traditions

It is the goal of this text to remind some and enlighten others of the origins and traditions of Japanese karate today. The objective is to build a better person that can live harmoniously with others.

Actually, there are so many interesting aspects to training in this art that you can easily do it for a lifetime. Unlike many other sports and activities that are only for the young, karate has no such restrictions. From our children to our seniors, men and women, all are encouraged to take up this fascinating art.

When American and other foreigners arrived in Japan after World War II and began training in the martial arts, they faced Japanese sensei who were battle-hardened combat veterans. To those sensei, most of what they taught was applied in real conflict and not just a matter of theory to them. You could see it in their eyes. The intensity, attitude and spirit made you feel that every class was preparing you for life or death. This was the samurai spirit of Japanese martial arts.

Since this was such a deadly and disabling art, a tremendous amount of emphasis was placed on having total respect for each other. It could be no other way; the art was too dangerous. Emphasis was on building the spirit, to face an opponent as if it were a matter of life and death and the enjoyment of your training. None of it was meant to be frivolous.

## Sharpen Your Skills

Beginners must spend hours practicing to improve their power and speed. Control is paramount. You must deliver a technique with full force, but you also have to control it and stop short of causing your opponent any injury. Delivering techniques as if it were a game of tag is a bad habit, so it's important that you always train seriously.

Even in controlled training in the dojo, accidents and injuries will occur. When this happens, you must stop and attend to the injury. However, in real encounters on the street, no one will stop for your injuries. That is why it's important to build your spirit so you can overcome adversity and to mentally prepare yourself to continue despite pain.

In training, emotion, especially anger, is not tolerated. You must control yourself, both mentally and physically. *"Mizo No Kokoro."* That is a phrase attributed to the Japanese samurai and today's martial artist. It means, "Having a mind like water." Like still water, you should show no emotion when facing an opponent. No emotion!

When training, treat every kick and punch thrown at you as serious, even life-threatening. Defend yourself accordingly. Build your technique and prepare yourself for real-life encounters. It is possible to go through your entire life without ever resorting to self-defense or violence, but it is best to be prepared.

As you study this text, we will preface each section with comments that will, hopefully, begin to build the warrior spirit of Japanese karate.

# Chapter I

# Body Weapons and Targets

There are probably far more ways to train your body to be an effective weapon than most people realize. Many of the methods we will demonstrate in this book are highly effective and serve as "equalizers" that will give you an advantage, despite of your size and strength.

The Japanese martial arts, in their original concept, were designed to immediately defeat an enemy. Such will be what we teach. To accomplish this, you will train to hit, kick, gouge, claw, bite and apply yourself in whatever manner necessary to defend yourself. The emphasis in this book will be defense against an attack. However, there is a section that explains what to do when faced with a truly dangerous situation. In this circumstance, you can take the initiative and attack. There's an old adage that states that a good offense is the best defense. Sometimes that is the best advice.

The more you train and the harder you train, the better you will become. We realize that most men and women will not devote the time to training that a professional will. If you are in the armed forces, law enforcement or any of the specialized units that require you to face hazardous situations — perhaps life threatening situations — then you must, of course, apply yourself far more diligently than the general public.

Finding a reputable school and qualified teacher of the martial arts is your best way to learn this art. If this is not possible — for whatever reason — or if you are already enrolled in a school and wish to supplement your training, set a schedule and practice. The more you train the better you become.

## Punching
## Tsuki
## or
## Zuki

Hitting with a closed fist requires proper technique so you do not damage your hand. The brazen, wild swings we see in films are not the proper way to hit. Also, karate punches differ from boxing, which has protective gloves and wrappings for your hands.

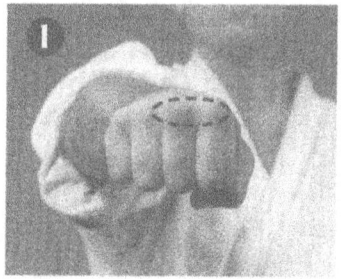 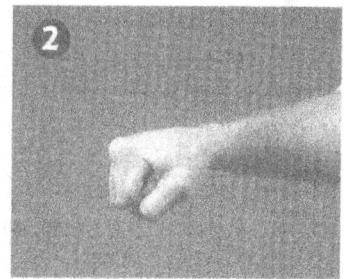

First, note that the contact surface of a fist/punch is the first two knuckles, as illustrated. Notice the straight alignment of the forearm. A straight wrist will deliver a much stronger punch and prevent injury.

To apply more muscle into the punch, your shoulder should be "seated" and not hyperextended. Illustration No. 1 shows the shoulder out, thereby neutralizing the pectoral muscles and others in the back. Illustration No. 2 shows the shoulder down, applying the pectoral muscle and adding more power to the punch.

Jabs, hook punches, U punches and other techniques are exceptions to this shoulder-seated rule. As you work on a body bag, you will begin to realize the difference. Because most people never throw a punch, we will start with the basics.

1 Extend one arm and keep the other at your side.

2 Begin to punch with the hand at your side. At the same time, start to draw back your extended hand.

3 Twist the punching hand into place and continue drawing the extended hand to your hip.

Karate blows have a twisting action to enhance the power. Also, keep your elbows and arms close to your body. Letting your elbows flare out will dissipate your power. This simple routine of standing and throwing punches is absolutely essential to building good punching habits.

Applying the same principles as you did for the punch, stand with one leg forward and rotate your punches. This is a forward stance, which will be covered in later text.

In the following photographs, the movements are similar to the initial way we demonstrated. After becoming accustomed to the motion, begin to feel your hips and lower body. Ultimately, you will learn to apply the strength of all of your muscles into the punch ... from your legs up. Continue this practice countless times. In fact, use it as a warm-up, and you will be building your muscles to deliver effective blows.

## Horse Stance
### Kiba-dachi

Another simple but necessary way to warm up is to practice your punches. The stance shown here (A), known as *kiba-dachi* (horse stance), is also covered in a later chapter. The purpose is to squat low and put stress on your legs. You are now getting a dual workout; both your arms and legs are

*Chapter 1 — Body Weapons and Targets*

developing. This, however, is not the way to stand in front of an opponent and attack. The proper use for this stance will be covered later. Use this for training only.

We'll now discuss how to deliver a punch with a forward step. Because most altercations involve movement, you will begin now to learn the maneuvers. This first one is simple. When you do it, strive for balance and practice as if your opponent has shifted out of range, forcing you to follow him.

*1* Start as shown. Your rear hand should rest on your hip, ready to deliver. Meanwhile, you will begin with your front leg forward.

*2* When you step, draw your heels close to each other for balance. As you step into the punch, widen the stance for balance as the blow lands. Practice this for now and we'll get into more detail later.

*3* To get the most power, shift all of your weight into the punch. As your front foot locks on the ground, your fist makes contact with your target.

## Straight Punch
Choku-zuki

Complete sequence *choku-zuki* from natural stance with hip rotation.

*Chapter 1 — Body Weapons and Targets*

The following pages will elude possible targets on body to attack and some of many "weapons" you can use. This illustration shows a defensive posture you can assume, from which you may apply your technique.

## Target Practice

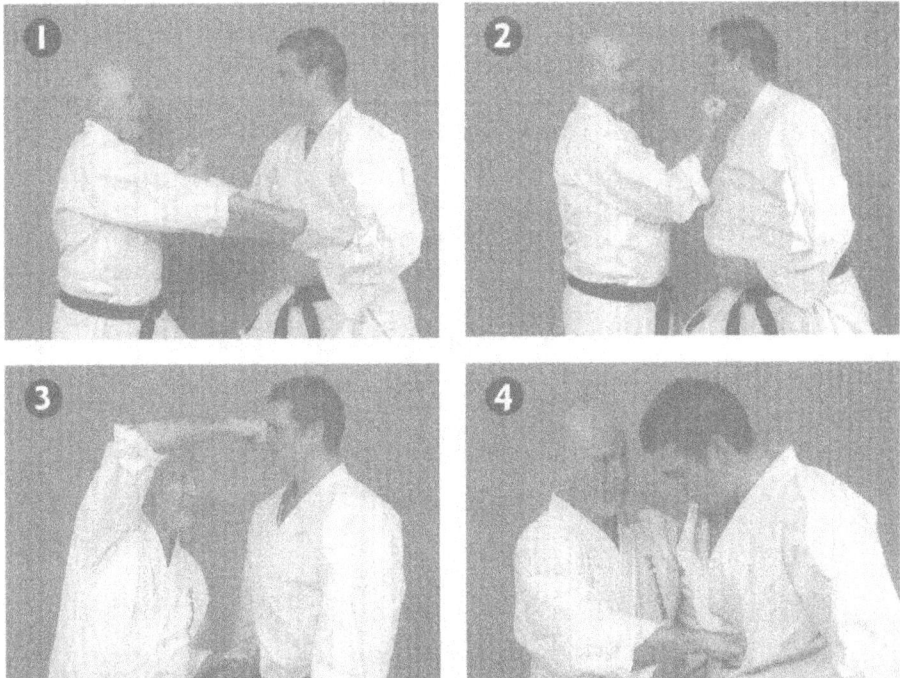

1 This is a straight punch *(choku zuki)* to the solar plexus.

2 Close-up of an upper cut or close punch *(ura zuki)*.

3 Double punch *(yama zuki)* or "U" punch *(morote zuki)*. Used to strike two targets simultaneously.

4 This is a hook punch *(kagi zuki)* which is a perfect weapon to use if your opponent is standing slightly to the side.

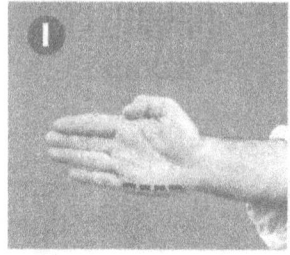 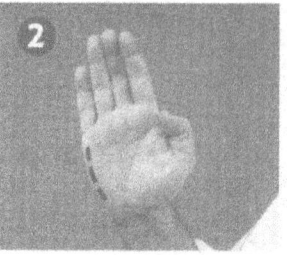 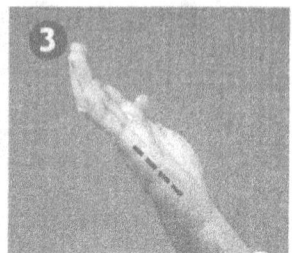

## Knifehand
## Shuto

This is a knifehand *(shuto)*. Notice that the hand is held ridged. The striking surface is the meaty portion of the bottom of the palm. The three illustrations illustrate this technique. Knifehand blows are not as familiar to countries outside of Asia. This technique is used to strike surfaces in which the narrow palm edge will fit better than a fist.

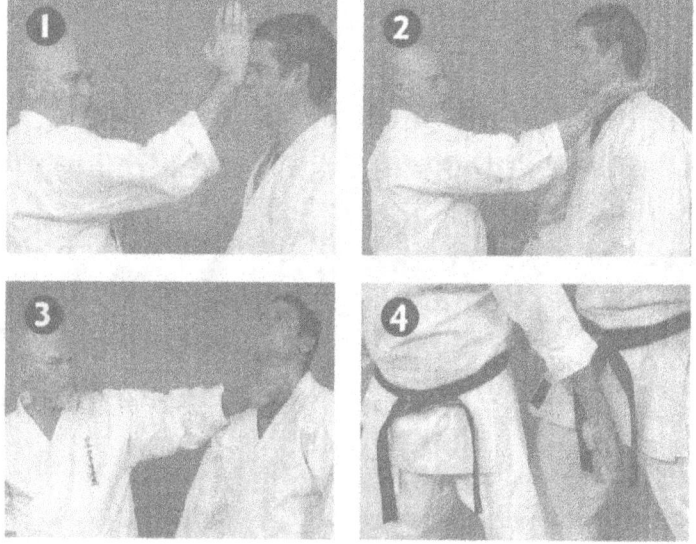

1 The overhand blow can be thrown directly to the forehead, between the eyes or to the bridge of the nose.

2 This is a circular or round strike to the neck and carotid artery.

Chapter 1 — Body Weapons and Targets

3 If your opponent is to your side, you may apply a backhand strike to vulnerable areas, such as the throat, nose, etc.

4 If your opponent is directly to your side, throw a downward chopping action to the groin.

CAUTION: *All blows can be extremely dangerous. Some can even be fatal. Use discretion. Apply only when you are in imminent danger of receiving serious injury.*

## Spearhand
## Nukite

When you throw a spear hand, use your fingertips to attack your opponent's eyes, throat, solar plexus, etc. One- and two-finger stabs to the eyes and clawing action with all of your fingers are variations.

1 This is the proper way to hold your hand. Notice how the fingers are extended and the thumb is clamped in tight.

2 This is a blow to the solar plexus.

3 A blow to the throat, using an upper-cut motion. When you strike with your fingers, make sure your knuckles are slightly bent. If too rigid, the fingers can buckle and break.

9

*Chapter 1 — Body Weapons and Targets*

Finger attacks are effective and require very little strength to apply.

## Finger Strikes
## Yubi Uchi

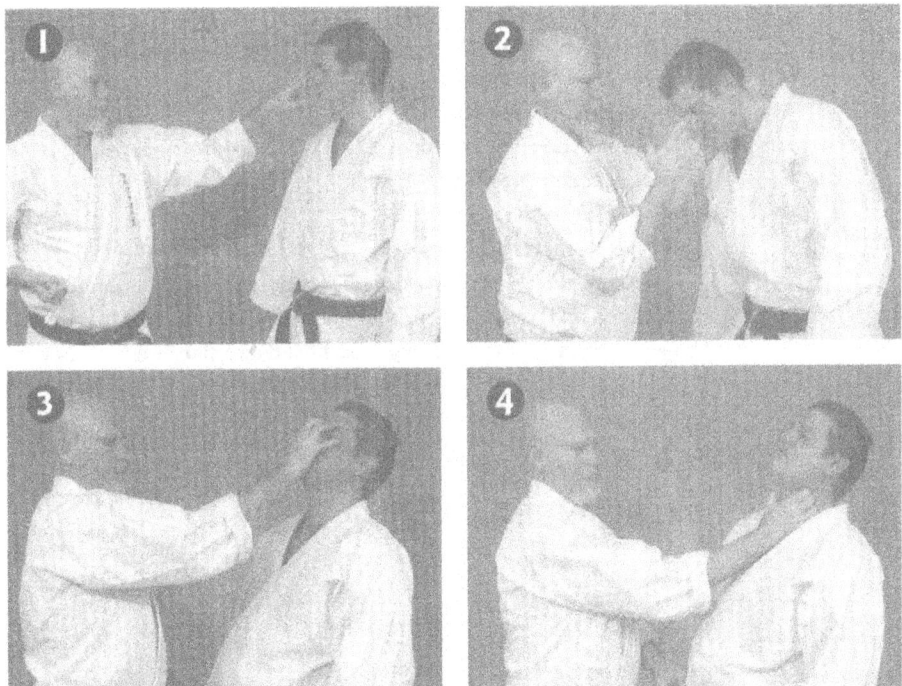

1 Two-finger attack *(nihon nukite)* to the eye.

2 Single finger *(nihon nukite)* to the eye.

3 Clawhand *(kumade)* gouging eyes and face.

4 Claw or vice grip *(kokou uchi)* grabbing the throat and clamping.

Again, all such attacks can be extremely harmful, even deadly. Therefore, use them with caution.

## Backfist
## Uraken

In karate training, you must develop many unusual ways to strike, depending on circumstances, the angle of your opponent and what is open for you to deliver.

What is recognized as the conventional way to stand in front of your opponent and throw a punch may not be appropriate. You must train to strike from any position, using your body weapons that will be the most effective.

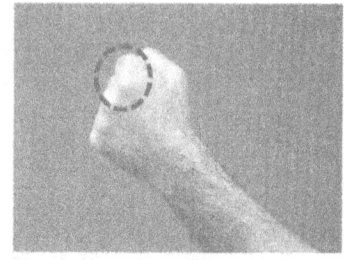

The backfist, which hits with the solid back part of the hand, is very effective and easy to learn. In the early stages of training, most beginners can deliver a stronger backfist than a punch.

1 A backfist can be applied to an opponent who is standing to your side, provided he is facing the same direction as you.

2 You can also throw a backfist when your opponent stands perpendicular to you.

3 You can throw a roundhouse or circular backfist to the side of an oppo-

Chapter 1 — Body Weapons and Targets

nent, too. Remember, a technique is used whenever an opening presents itself. Finding the right technique for the right opening is why you learn so many varied strikes of Japanese karate.

## Hammer Fist Strikes
### Kentusi

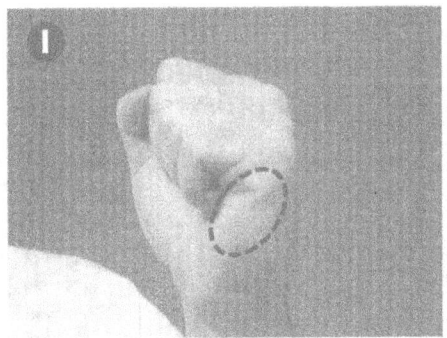 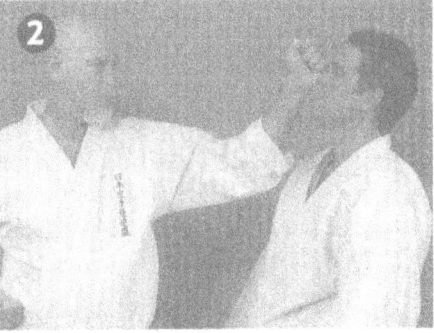

1 The hammer strike uses the bottom of the fist with a pounding force, not unlike the action of a hammer. This blow is effective and less damaging to a beginner's fist. When learned properly, the hammer blow becomes another weapon for your arsenal.

2 The bridge of the nose is one of the possible targets to strike. Notice that the motion is an overhand, downward strike *(otoshi)*.

## Hammer Fist Strikes
## Kentusi

*continued*

1 You can use a back swing action to strike the rib cage, solar plexus or other targets.

2 Another downward hammer strike to the side of the face, temple, etc.

3 If your opponent is off balance or he is diving toward you with his head down, the hammer fist at the back of the neck is very effective and can be extremely dangerous.

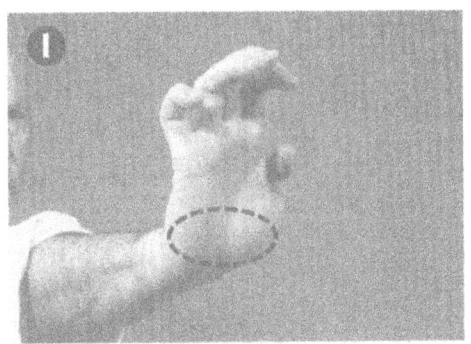

# Palm Heel Strike
## Teisho Uchi

1 When you throw a palm heel strike, pull your fingers back and strike with the solid part of your palm. Depending on the circumstances (angle of opponent, your position), a palm heel can be very effective.

2 Paul Godshaw swings the technique from the outside, so it moves inward toward the target.

3 Here, Godshaw demonstrates how to throw the technique when the target is the groin.

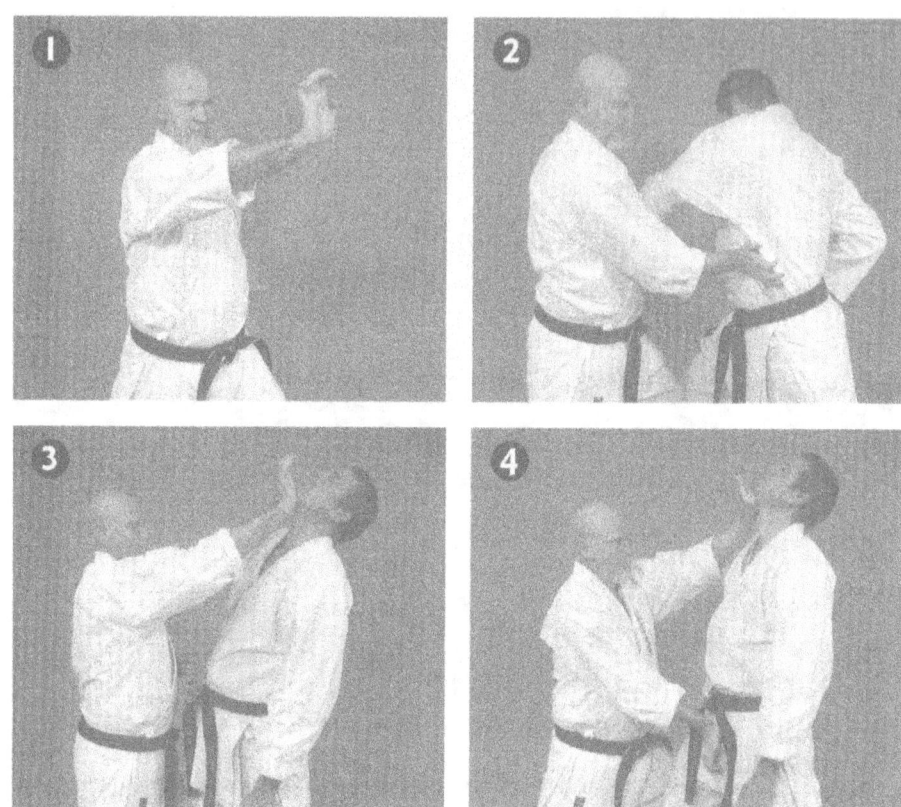

**Palm Heel Strike**
Teisho Uchi
*continued*

1 This is one of the most common strikes, driving upward into an opponent in front of you.

2 When an opening presents itself, take advantage of it. Here, Paul Godshaw drives the strike upward into the soft ribcage.

3 An upward driving strike is effective against an opponent's chin. A more dangerous move would be upward into the nose.

4 A double-palm heel to an opponent's groin and chin.

*Chapter 1 — Body Weapons and Targets*

## Ridgehand Strike
## Haito Uchi

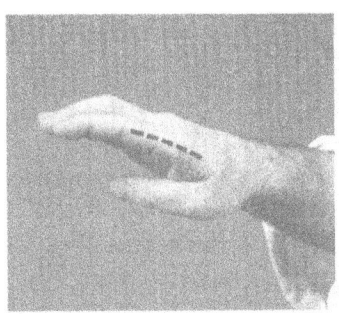 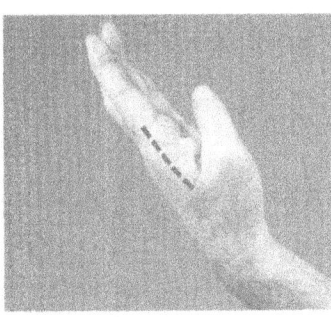

This strike is used to penetrate narrow surfaces, such as under the chin, etc. It is used both palm up and palm down, depending on which opportunity presents itself. Fold your thumb against your palm so you won't damage it when striking.

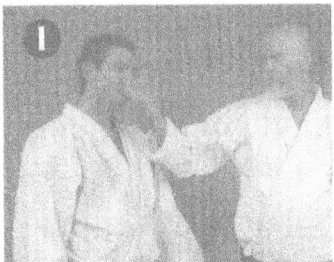 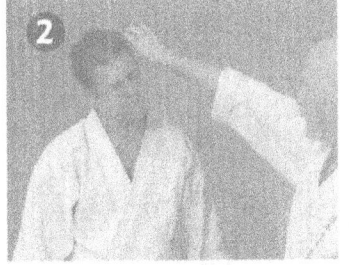

1 When you are sideways to your opponent, throw a quick strike upward under the nose (or throat). Keep your thumb tucked into your palm so you won't get hurt.

2 You can throw a ridgehand to the side of the temple or even the neck.

3 A ridgehand to the groin is quick and effective. The narrow edge of the hand strikes upward and between the legs.

## Knuckle Strikes
## Nakuru

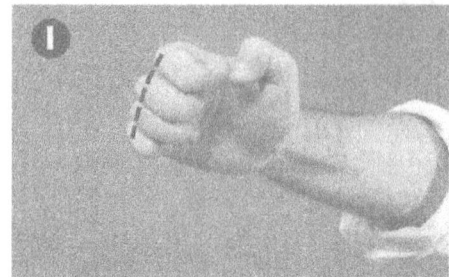

1 As illustrated, fold your fingers back, using your knuckles to strike at the targets.

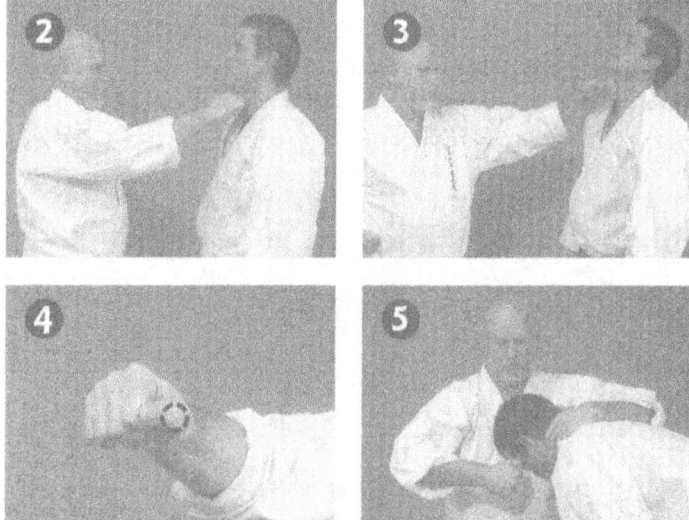

2 An example of this technique to the throat.
3 Different hand positions can still do damage to vulnerable areas.
4 This is a thumb-knuckle strike.
5 A thumb-knuckle strike to the temple.

*Chapter 1 — Body Weapons and Targets*

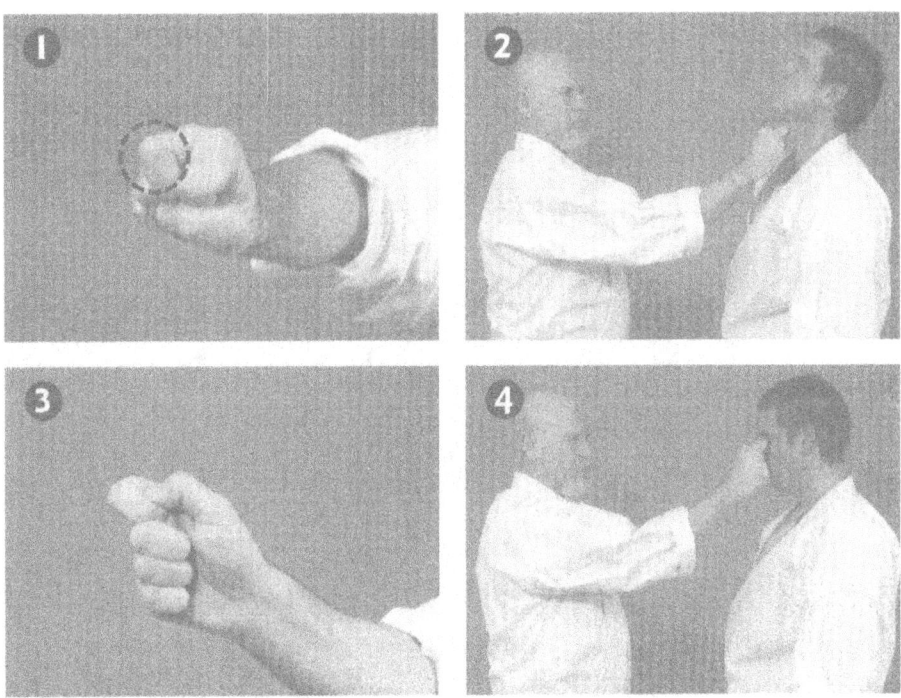

*1* A middle-knuckle strike.

*2* Strike to the throat, eyes or temple, depending on the angle of the opponent.

*3* This is a forefinger-knuckle strike.

*4* In addition to the attack illustrated, this knuckle can be used against the solar plexus.

Most knuckle strikes are interchangeable and even a person of smaller stature and strength can cause extreme damage. These can be dangerous, but can be used when you are in real- life, serious situations.

## Elbow Strikes

### Empi Uchi

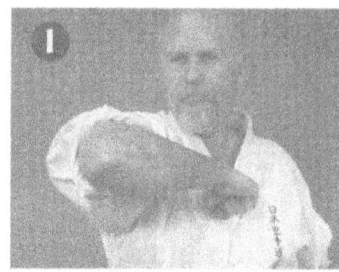

*1* This is a circular motion, hitting your opponent in the face.

*2* The upward elbow blow is used to strike under your opponent's chin and other targets.

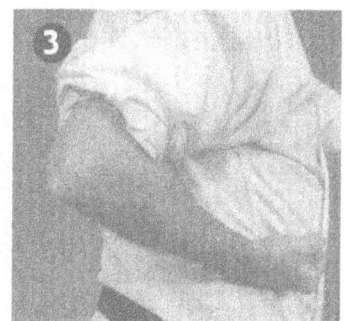
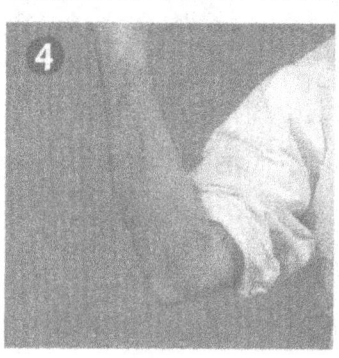
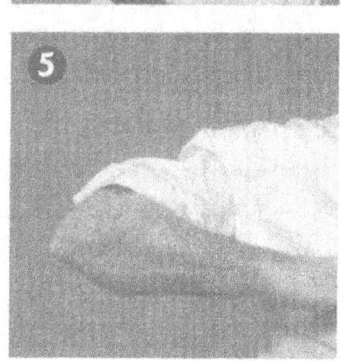

*3* Rear elbows can be used for attackers standing directly behind you.

*4* The downward elbow can be thrown to your opponent's back or his neck when he lunges with his head down.

*5* The side elbow blow can be used if your opponent is directly to your side. Throw it at his face or solar plexus.

*Chapter 1 — Body Weapons and Targets*

## Examples of Targets to Strike with Elbows

*1* Circular blows can be thrown to the chin, face, temple, etc.

*2* An upward strike to the chin.

*3* A backward strike to the solar plexus. This can also be thrown to the face, etc.

*4* A sideways strike to the solar plexus. Note, for more power, this strike can be augmented with your other hand.

*5* The downward strike comes in handy when your attacker dives or you find him bent over in front of you.

*Chapter 1 — Body Weapons and Targets*

# Kicking Techniques
## Keri Waza

Kicks are, in most instances, stronger than hand blows, because the legs are so much more powerful than the arms. Kicking also gives you the advantage of distance and can be an equalizer when facing opponents who are bigger and stronger than you.

Kicking requires good balance, because you stand on one leg when delivering the technique. In real-life altercations, effective kicks should be kept to the lower part of the body. The higher you kick at an opponent, the harder it is to balance.

This section covers the fundamental kicks that can be strong and accurate. Face kicks, jump kicks and spinning kicks require far more practice and balance and are not used as often in street encounters.

## Front Kick
### Mae Geri

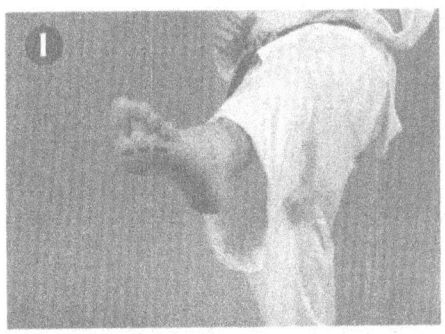 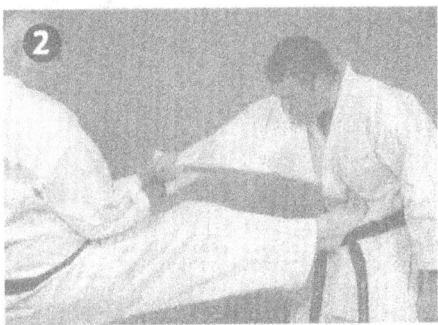

1 When barefoot, the kick is applied with the ball of the foot. With shoes on, it is the toe of the shoe. For a variation, you can use the instep.

2 This is an example of a front kick to the stomach. Other targets can be the kneecap, groin or legs. In fact, you can go for any target that presents itself. The front kick is possibly the strongest and fastest kick you can learn and apply.

## Side Kick
## Yoko Geri

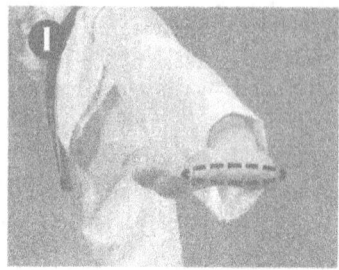 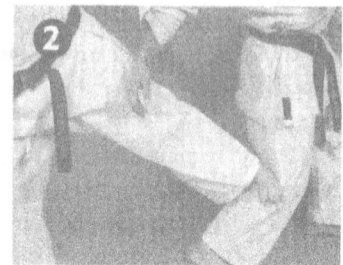

1 To throw this kick properly barefoot, strike your target with the side of your foot. If you are wearing shoes, use the edge of your heel.

2 An example of the side kick to an opponent's knee joint.

## Back Kick
## Ushiro Geri

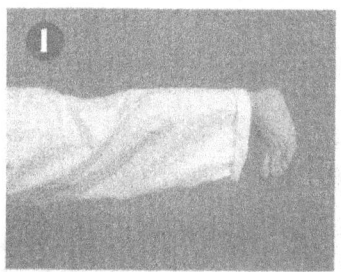 

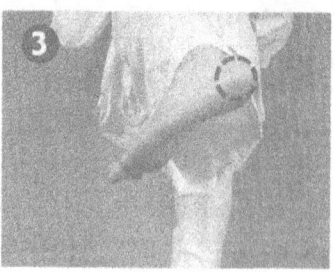

1 Use your heel to kick anyone attacking from the rear.

2 Here is an example of a kick to the groin.

3 This is a close-up look at the strong part of the heel. This is where you want to make contact.

## Round Kick
## Mawashi Geri

Although it is a bit difficult to see the proper technique here, we will present good, basic training later on that will help you develop the roundhouse kick.

*1* You should strike your target with the ball of your foot, and the kick is delivered in a round or circular motion.

*2* An example of a kick to the stomach. You can also go for the legs, knees or groin.

## Knee Kick
## Hiza Geri

This is used for close-in fighting, much like elbows. This is used often because many people get into a clinch during altercations.

*1* A knee strike.

*2* A knee strike to the face. The most common target is the groin.

*Japanese Karate: A 'Warrior's Spirit*

# HID POWCr

One of the most important principles of Japanese karate: "Using your hips properly."

A tremendous amount of emphasis is placed on this principle. But it's not just karate. The same can be said for other martial arts, too. The reason you put your hips into a technique is to generate more power, whether you're striking with your hands or using your legs.

For example, your leg muscles are much stronger than your arms. Therefore, if you can transmit the power of the leg muscle into your hand strikes, you will create far more power.

The hips regulate all of this power, and the technique is transmitted from the ground up, right through the feet, toes, legs, hips, back and arm muscles.

1 Paul Godshaw demonstrates how to begin using your hips. Note that his hips are half turned away from the target.

2 Here he throws a technique with his hips open.

3 Then he twists his hips into the target and releases his arm into the punch.

This can be done with a partner, body bag, or even a hanging shirt or a jacket. Your goal is to learn to twist into an oppo- nent/target. Begin by practicing the twist hundreds — if not thousands — of times until you can actually feel the leg thrust from the ground up, right into the punch.

As you learn more of this art, you will find that applying the proper hip action into any strike will add for more power than arms and shoulders alone. Eventually, you will apply this same principle into your kicks. The standing leg, via your hips, will transmit power to the kick. Again, practicing on a body bag or pad will help you to develop this "hip power."

## Target Practice

Karate techniques can be dangerous and harmful to a partner; therefore, use extreme caution when you practice. There should be absolutely no contact. Of course, blocks will require some contact, but the counterstrike and kicks should be controlled. The goal is to deliver the technique with maximum force but with complete control.

Of course, slight contact against a loose uniform may be OK, but any contact to the face can cause injury. Therefore, we recommend you always practice slowly at first, without full force, until you have complete control of your techniques. Initially, practice for accuracy. Once you have that down, add the speed and power as your skill level increases.

Target practice against a body bag or striking pad is the best way to begin building power. With a bag or pad, you can feel your force as you advance in training and develop the necessary strikes, kicks and stances.

Mounting a body bag or pad is a way to practice without a partner. However, if a partner is available, have him hold a striking pad while he moves about. This will add to your mobility and maneuvering. In ancient times, before bags were developed, martial artists threw kicks and punches against a *makiwara*, which is a flexible board buried in the ground. Even today, many karate practitioners use a makiwara to develop power.

Another rather unusual way to develop your technique — and hip application — is to hang a simple towel in a doorway. This gives you a target to focus on and will help to develop speed and power.

Focus, which can be defined as complete concentration, is another important aspect of Japanese karate training. It's vital that you focus your mind and energy on the techniques. Focus all of your power — as described in the hip movement — into each block, strike and kick. Focus on the situation, what is about to happen, and your anticipated response. Mentally prepare yourself at all times. Therefore, if you're ever a victim of an unexpected attack, you can immediately focus on your response.

These ideas and tips are all designed to make you a better martial artist. However, remember that it is your spirit and mindset that will be your strongest weapon.

After you have trained yourself to deliver punches and attacks from the basic position, it's time to begin learning from a more "prepared" position.

*1* Assume a fighting stance. Your legs should be slightly apart, balanced and your arms ready. From here, you can jab, punch, kick, and/or move in, back or sideways. This is the ideal stance. Find a position suitable for your body style.

2 Practice sliding forward with a jab.

3 Follow-up with a counter punch. Don't forget to use the driving force of your hips and legs.

This is the simple one-two punch. You should develop this to be quick and powerful.

## Backfist Strikes and Knifehand Strikes

*1* Fighting stance

*2* Draw your hand back for a backhand blow. The draw back and delivery must be done with the utmost speed, so that your opponent doesn't have time to defend.

*3* Snap the backhand into the body, face or neck. Go for whatever target presents itself. Use your hips and legs for more power.

*4-5* This is the same technique as the backhand, except now you are practicing a chop.

## Adding Combinations

*1* Assume a fighting stance.

*2* Slide in and throw a front-hand chop.

*3* Follow up with another chop. You may now begin to add combinations, mixing punches, chops, kicks, etc.

*4-5* Here is an example of a palm heel strike.

*Chapter 1 — Body Weapons and Targets*

*1* Assume a stance. Practice with different stances, such as having your legs forward, standing to one side, etc.

*2* Use an elbow strike for close-in situations.

*3* Assume a back or side position.

*4* Practice a backward elbow blow. Also try side blows, etc.

Remember, you have a variety of strikes to learn. Mix them up and practice them all. Use combinations, different stances and, if possible, a partner. Maneuver as you practice.

## Developing Strong Kicks

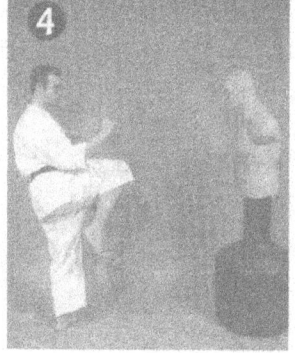

Kicking requires good balance, so we will start with basic positions to help you learn proper balance and learn how to develop power in your kicks.

*1* Stand facing your target. Your feet should be together, back straight and your knees slightly bent.

*2* Draw your leg up to prepare the muscles for the technique. This is much like drawing back a bow.

*3* Snap the kick out, hitting the target with the ball of your foot.

*4* Draw your kick back sharply.

*5* Return your leg to the floor.

*Chapter 1 — Body Weapons and Targets*

**KEY POINTS**
- Don't stand stiff-legged. Your knees should be slightly bent to provide some cushioning.
- Keep your back straight. Bending over makes the kick more difficult to throw.
- Although you learn in stages, you must ultimately learn to kick in one swift movement.
- Drawing your kick back quickly will prevent your opponent from catching it.
- Don't scoop your kick. If you scoop or kick without drawing your leg up, you are not applying all of your muscles. Furthermore, your kicks will be slower. You can practice drawing your leg up by kicking over an object such as a chair.

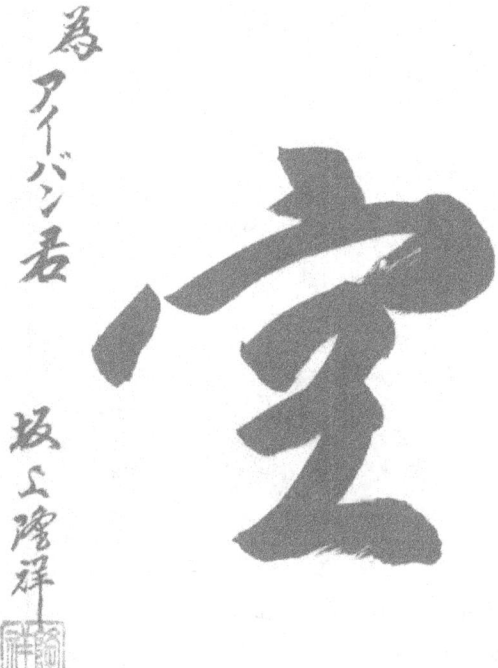

"EMPTY"

Ryusho Sakagami
to Dan Ivan

## Side Kicks

As the name implies, this kick comes from the side. During sessions which we will discuss later, you and an opponent will be maneuvering for position. While doing this, you will find opportunities to throw a side kick and all of the kicks you will eventually learn. It all depends on where you or your opponent moves.

1 All kicks require almost the same basics. Your back should be straight and your knees slightly bent.

2 Draw your leg up to prepare the muscle for the kick.

*Chapter 1 — Body Weapons and Targets*

**3** Deliver the kick sharply to the target.

**4** Draw your leg back.

**5** Return your leg to the floor position.

    This is the basic way to practice. Like all of your kicks, however, this movement must be delivered in one swift move. Snap the kick out and bring it back as quickly as possible. Your leg should just be a blur.

    Remember, the striking surface is the edge of your foot. There are two types of sidekicks: thrust and snap. For the purpose of this text, apply your kick with a pushing hip action. More details will be addressed after you have learned mechanics and balance.

*"KNOWLEDGE LIKE A MOUNTAIN, HEART LIKE WATER"*

*Ito Kazuo,
Kodohan 9th Dan*

## Round Kick

A round kick is done in a circular motion, and it is also developed to hit a target whenever an opportunity presents itself.

1 Assume a fighting stance. Let us note something here. Eventually, you will develop your own style. However, this stance is one of the better you can assume, because you are aligned toward your opponent. This puts you in the best position to deliver almost all of your kicks and blows. Of course, skilled fighters can change their stances instantly. Using many

*Chapter 1 — Body Weapons and Targets*

different stances confuses their opponents. The beginner is a different story, and that is why we recommend the stance shown.

**2** Prepare for this kick by lifting your leg parallel to the floor, as shown.

**3** Twist your hips in and toward the target. Then you can deliver the kick.

**4** Return your leg to the starting position and bring your hips back.

**5** Return your leg to the floor.

Bringing your leg back and holding it up are basic moves. Once you master these, you will perform more difficult moves, which will help you develop additional power and balance. Eventually, in all of your kicks, you may step forward or sideways. In fact, you will eventually be going in different directions to follow an opponent. For now, practice this basic way

**37**

## Back Kick

Learn this kick so you can apply it when attacked from behind. Also, as we mentioned, during altercations or friendly sparring with an opponent, you could find yourself in many different positions. Learning this kick gives you one more option. This is especially important because you are most vulnerable from the rear. After you throw this kick, it's vital that you return to a defensive position as quickly as possible. Needless to say, all kicks must be learned properly.

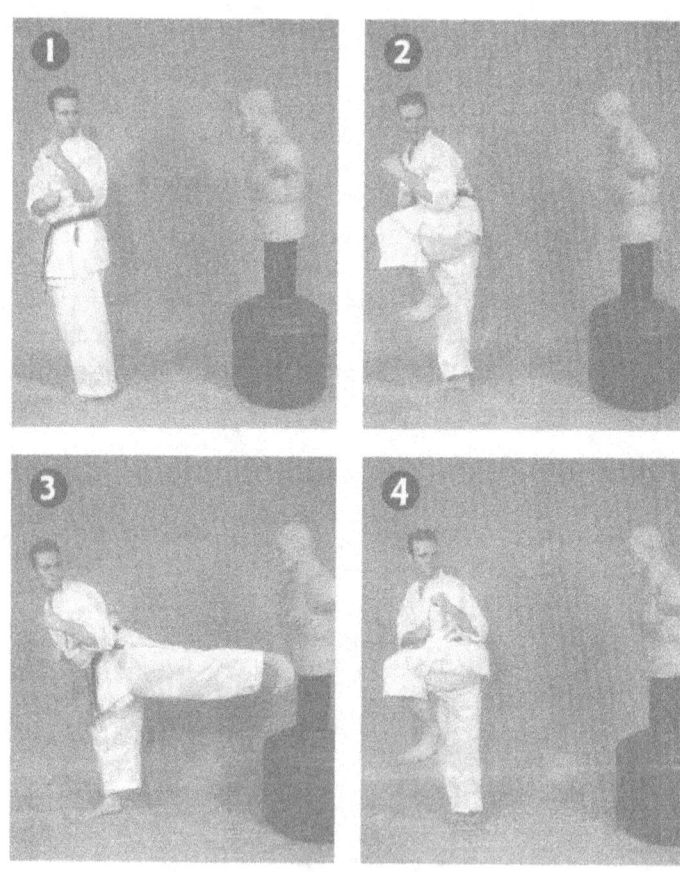

*Chapter 1 — Body Weapons and Targets*

*1* You'll notice that the same principles that we discussed earlier are evident here. Notice that his back is straight, his legs are slightly bent and he is looking over his shoulder to the target.

*2* Draw your leg up to prep the muscle.

*3* Deliver the heel to the target as shown.

*4* Draw your leg back to the position shown.

*5* Return your leg to the floor as shown.

The mechanics of all the kicks are much the same. For example, you draw your leg up to prep the muscle, you deliver the kick and return the kick sharply back to the floor. Remember, however, when you learn the kicks well, you should throw all of them fast. There will be no pauses between the steps. When you throw them at full speed, they will just be a blur, and it will be hard for anyone to defend against them.

## Strike Routines

If you have a partner and striking pads or other implements, you can improvise and practice combinations. Have your partner move around a bit so you have to follow him. Practice your strikes, kicks and maneuvers, using any combination you see.

You should also have your partner thrust at you as if he were attacking you. This will give you the opportunity to learn how to avoid these attacks and practice counters.

Remember, you need focus, balance and hip power. These are the elements you need at the beginning. Start slowly and then build your speed and accuracy.

*1* While his partner holds the focus mitts, Paul Godshaw assumes a ready position.

*2* He throws a right.

*3* He finishes with a left reverse punch.

*Chapter 1 — Body Weapons and Targets*

1 Paul Godshaw shows some of the other combinations you can throw. He begins with a left open-hand strike.

2 He comes back with a second open-hand technique.

3 He concludes with a nasty uppercut.

1 Paul Godshaw mixes it up by first throwing a front kick.
2 Godshaw concludes with a blistering backfirst.

# Chapter 2

# Stances and Footwork

Following are some important points pertaining to stances and footwork:

The stances and footwork in Japanese karate have been carefully analyzed and geometrically calculated to obtain maximum efficiency for each particular use.

You can compare stances with a bent leg to a suppressed spring. When a technique is executed, the spring is released and the power of the leg is transmitted into the technique.

Some may see the stances as either "offensive" or "defensive." Actually, most of these positions can be applied either way.

Stances should be used under the right circumstances and conditions, considering your opponent, situation and environment.

- Your body type is also important. You will find some stances more suitable to you than others, depending on your size, weight and so on.
- You must be flexible and train to make transitions from stance to stance, depending on all of the above.
- You must train to move about freely, applying the proper stance and technique when the opportunity presents itself.
- Practice moving in all directions: side to side, forward, backward and diagonally. With experience, you will learn to adjust to the situation.
- Posture is important, too. This art uses kicking along with striking. Thus, you must stand erect as much as possible. Leaning or bending to an extreme will make it more difficult to apply leg kicks. When necessary, of course, you can duck, bend and dodge to avoid attacks. If you do this,

spring back upright and straight so you can kick effectively as quickly as possible.
- As you become more proficient, you will acquire the skills to maneuver, find positions to attack an opponent and avoid his attack.
- To understand stances and footwork more, attend a karate tournament and watch the advanced students engage in free fighting. Fighters will move about, looking for openings, maneuvering, attacking and defending. You can learn quite a bit from watching free fighting or any advanced class of a reputable school and instructor.
- The three stances depicted here are considered formal positions, and they are usually used prior to starting your class, bowing or fighting an opponent.

**1** This stance is called *heisoku dachi* and is usually used while being addressed by your sensei.

**2** This is *musubi dachi*. Note how his feet are slightly apart and his hands are at his side. This is usually the stance used for bowing.

*Chapter 2 — Stances and Footwork*

3 *Hachiji dachi,* also known as the ready stance, is usually done after the bow to the opponent is completed and just before the fight begins.

*Zenkutsu dachi* is considered a "power stance." Look closely at Alan Godshaw. Notice how he has more weight over his front leg. This should be about 70 percent of his body weight. From this stance, you could kick from the rear leg. The front hand can be used for a jab and the rear hand for a counter punch. When punching or striking, push off with your rear leg, transmitting this leg power into the strike. A slightly shorter version of this forward stance is a common free-fighting position.

**Forward Stance**
Zenkutsu Dachi

1 Alan Godshaw demonstrates an "on-guard" position. His hands are ready to strike or defend.

2 This is a side view of the same stance. Notice that his upper body is slightly turned, offering his opponent a lesser target but also allowing important hip action for any strike or kick.

## Back Stance
### Kokutsu Dachi

In this stance, your weight should be more distributed over the back leg (about 70 percent). This is also used more for defense, although many attacks can be initiated from this position.

*1, 2* Note that his back foot is turned for a better grip. When withdrawing from an attack, turn the foot for a strong recovery. Good defensive position and kicking are easier with the front leg.

## Immovable Stance
### Fudo Dachi

This stance is a powerful fighting stance, especially for upper-body strikes. Note how his legs are positioned much like they would be in the forward stance. The exception is the back leg is bent and the front leg is turned lightly inward.

## Horse Stance
## Kiba Dachi

This wide-legged stance is used to shift sideways and evade attacks. This stance proves useful if standing with your back to a wall or some other obstruction and can't move backward from an attack. In this case, you'll have to shift sideways from the attacker. You may also shift back and turn into this stance when attacked, allowing your opponent to pass you. Counterattacks from this position are limited; therefore, immediately after you defend or shift away from an attack, make a transition into a forward stance or any of the other attack positions you have learned.

*1, 2* These photos illustrate two angles to help you better understand the stance. Remember, you also learn to punch from this stance, but that is only done while exercising because that will develop stronger leg muscles.

## Box Stance
### Shiko Dachi

This stance is much like the horse stance except the stress on the legs is somewhat relieved because you turn your feet outward. This makes the stance a bit more maneuverable. Apply it much like the horse stance in attack and defense.

## Cat Stance
### Neko Ashi Dachi

In the cat stance, the weight is almost entirely on the rear leg. This leaves the front leg free to kick. It's also a highly maneuverable stance and perhaps more defensive than the others. From this stance, it is easy to make transitions to other stances when blocking, striking and kicking.

**1, 2** These photos provide two views to better understand the stance. As with all your stances, the legs are bent. Notice how the front leg is prepared on the ball of the foot. Practice vari-

*Chapter 2 — Stances and Footwork*

ous defenses and attacks from this stance. For example, you might throw a front kick, a front hand jab, drop into a forward stance and counter punch.

## Half-Moon Stance
### Hangetsu Dachi

When you do the *hangetsu* stance, you'll keep both of your legs close together and bend your knees. See illustrations 1 and 2 below. In many of the Japanese and Okinawan forms, this stance is used. However, for the taller Westerners, it is not as readily utilized.

In learning this art, consideration must be given to the body structure of the founders of the art. They were a bit smaller in stature and could adapt to these stances easier. This stance would be good if you are fighting "close in;" perhaps your opponent rushed you. You can use this stance to drive your blows up and into the target. So it seems that this stance is best suited for close-in fighting.

## Hour Glass Sanchin Dachi

This stance is similar to hangetsu, but the legs are much closer together. See illustrations 1 and 2.

There is a form called sanchin that stresses dynamic tensions and utilizes this stance. Besides being a training form for dynamic tension, you can see that it would work very well if you were forced into an extreme close-in fight. If that happened, you could realize the use of your leg power by dropping into the sanchin stance and driving your blows upward into your opponent.

For sanchin and hangetsu, you can better appreciate the technique by standing very close to your body bag and practice striking from either of these stances.

Practice all of your strikes and kicks on a body bag or pad to better understand how to build your power and technique.

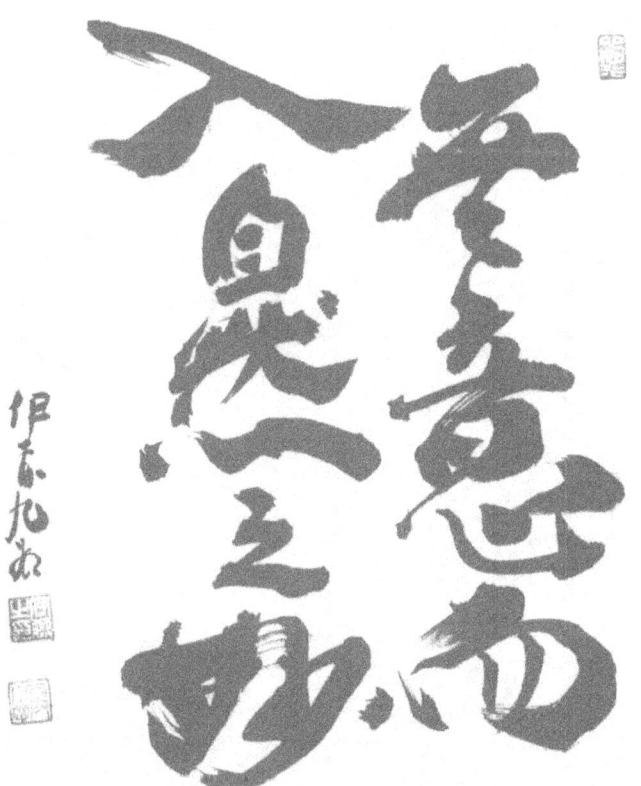

"BE NATURAL, NOT GREEDY"

*Ito Kazuo, Kodokan 9th Dan*

# Chapter 3

# Blocks and Evasion

In Japanese karate, the arms and legs are used for specific attack techniques. Therefore, the blocks and evasion techniques that you learn must teach you how to defend against such attacks.

When blocking, it's important to have the same *kime* (focus) that you would use in your strikes and kicks. Attacks will usually come at you forcefully, so you must learn to apply the block with the same energy.

Evasion is as important as the block. The primary principle behind evading, maneuvering or footwork is to nullify the force of the attack. As an example, if you are attacked with a lunge punch, you should draw back and away from the force of this punch, thereby dissipating the power. Standing toe-to-toe could work against you if your opponent is stronger than you.

With an evasive technique and the proper block, you now have two things working in your favor. Sometimes, blocking only will suffice. Other times, evasion only will suffice. If you can use them both properly, you will be far more effective.

Blocks, stances, evasions are all interchangeable. It really depends on factors such as:

- Environment. You could find yourself outside with lots of space, in close quarters and no room to move, or on a slippery surface or rough terrain.
- The size and strength of your opponent.
- The number of attackers.
- Finally, is it a friend that is angry or is it a stranger that you can't take chances with?

Most occasions will call for an evasive movement back and away from the attack. Some, however, may require you to move toward your opponent. Of course, before you decide, you have to consider all of the factors mentioned above.

When applying a block/evasive maneuver, you have to know how to do much more than just move backward. It's also imperative that you learn how to move at all angles.

We also recommend that you practice karate shadow boxing. As you know, this is vitally important to a boxer. It should be just as important to you.

Assume you have an imaginary opponent punching at you. Practice moving to all directions, applying the various blocks you have used. Do the same with a kicking scenario. Eventually, you should defend against combinations of punches and kicks. And don't forget to throw those counterstrikes. If you have a partner, practice together, using the utmost safety and caution.

## Upward Block
### Age like

1 The upward block is done to protect against face punches and overhand blows. To execute this properly, use your forearm surface to block. Keep your fist higher than your elbow. This angle allows you more strength in your arm. You can strengthen this block by bringing your arm from the hip area upward and diagonally across your body. Make sure that your arm sweeps across your face to catch the punch and direct it up and away. Using the forward stance, pull back as you apply the block.

Chapter 3 — Blocks and Evasion

2 This can be used to defend against body and face attacks. This block swings from the inside, across your body and deflects the blow outward. This is good for those blows that come at you in roundhouse or hooking style. This is demonstrated with a hangetsu stance, which is excellent for close-in tactics.

3 The outside forearm block is applied by bringing your arm from the outside — across your body or face — to deflect the punch. This is used with a cat stance. Note that your opposite hand is prepared to counter punch, and the front foot is ready to counter kick.

**Inside Forearm Block**
Uchi Uke

**Outside Forearm Block**
Soto Uke

*Japanese Karate: A Warrior's Spirit*

### Downward Block
### Gedan Uke

*1* This is used against a body blow or kick. The defender pulls back and twists his body as he blocks with his entire forearm. The block is executed by striking downward from across the body. This is done in a forward stance while pulling away from the attack.

### Downward Hooking Block
### Gedan Kake Uke

*2* This is an inside down block using the opposite side of your forearm to deflect a kick or low punch to the body. The block comes from outside and across the body.

### "X" Block
### Juji Uke

*3* The "X" block, which features the strength of both arms crossed to provide additional power, is used to trap or block a kick or low blow directed at your body. You can also jam a kick by stepping toward your opponent and executing an "X" block. If your opponent has extended his leg, it will be more difficult to block the kick. In this photo, the martial artist is in the sanchin stance. Remember, from this stance, you can also hold your legs together to avoid a low kick to the groin.

*Chapter 3 — Blocks and Evasion*

1 To execute the sweep block, use the palm of your hand to sweep punches away. Assume a back stance' and practice bringing your hand from high outside so that it moves across your face. Meanwhile, pull back into a stance.

2 The high "X" block is used for overhead blows and high punches. It is considered a "sacrifice" block if used to defend against an overhead blow with a club or hard object. Here, the block is shown while pulling back to a forward stance. Remember, evading helps to nullify the power of the attack. If your arms are strong, this will provide greater power against weapons.

3 When you execute the backhand sweep block, you use the back of your hand to deflect blows to the head. This is especially good for hooking or roundhouse attacks. Practice this by pulling back into your stance while bringing your arm up and across your face, deflecting outward.

**Sweep Block**
Nagashi like

**High "X" Block**
Jodan Juji Like

**Backhand Sweep Block**
Haishu like

## Palm Heel Block
Taisho like

1 The palm heel block deflects a blow upward. This is also good for striking up and under an arm when someone grabs you. Of course, you'd pull back into a stance while doing this.

2 This is a palm heel block deflecting across the body while pulling back diagonally. Palm heel techniques also work well as counter strikes.

## Chicken Head Block
Keito like

3 An ox block or "chicken head block" deflects upward with the edge of your hand. In this example, it is applied utilizing the cat stance. This technique may be used at any height. You can use it to stop low blows or strikes to the face.

*Chapter 3 — Blocks and Evasion*

**4** The double palm heel block features two blocks thrown simultaneously. It may be used to deflect kicks or punches. You should practice this wit a one-two action. First, block high. Then, assume that a kick is coming and block low. Use your imagination to conceive your own combinations to defend against.

**5** To execute the catch block or scooping block, pull back to allow your opponent's kick to extend. Then, clamp down on his foot or leg. You should have one hand on the bottom and one on top. Once you have a solid grasp on the kick, you can upset or throw your opponent by pushin or twisting.

### Double Palm Heel Block
RyoTeisho
Oshi Age Uke

### Scooping Block
Sukui Uke

**KEY POINTS FOR PRACTICE**

- Basic blocking can be practiced alone. Use exaggerated movements to build your technique. This also trains the muscles to remember the movements.
- Blocks have a "twisting" action; this adds impetus at the time of contact with the attacker.
- Most of the blocks demonstrated utilize the bone edge of your forearm. For example, forearm blocks, upward blocks and down blocks.
- Powerful blocks applied with focus can cause significant damage to an attacker's arms and legs, thus discouraging further attacks.
- Remember, evasion is critical. Practice evading to all directions. Sometimes, you will not be able to move back, so you must be able to move to the side or to various angles.
- When blocking with one hand, always draw the other hand into a position that prepares your counter. Study your body weapons.
- You can even practice blocks against a body bag or pad to develop strength in your blocks.
- In basic practice, you learn to react to attacks while your arms are at your sides and you are standing still. Normally, attacks come without warning. By starting from this position, you will build your reactions. As you advance, you will learn to defend and attack from a more ready position.
- Stances, footwork, blocks and evasion all work together. As we stressed, these are interchangeable. Practice stances and evasion by gliding over the floor smoothly. Keep your body erect. Build your skill so you will be able to move about freely to all positions. Practice moving back first. Then, quickly change directions. Reverse directions while you are practicing against imaginary opponents.
- It's important to be flexible in your ankles, knees and hips. This will help you to acquire more skilled movements. Remember that the hips are as critical when applied to blocks as they are to strikes and kicks.

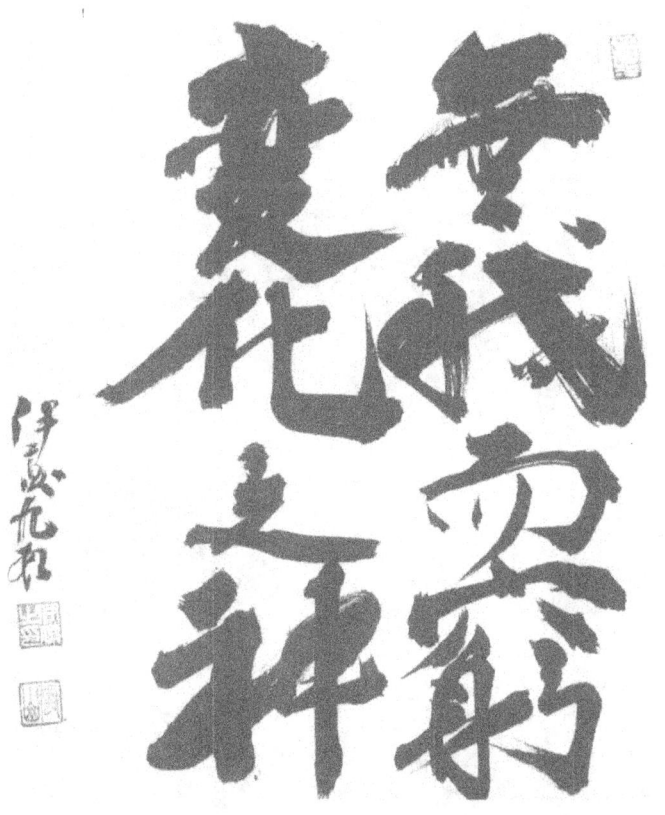

*"DO YOUR BEST WITHOUT EXPECTING ANY REWARD. THAT'S THE BEST TECHNIQUE."*

*Ito Kazuo
Kodohan, 9th Dan*

# Chapter 4

# Self-Defense Techniques

The techniques and combinations of Japanese karate are endless. Although today, in modern times, this art has a heavy emphasis on sport, it still remains basically self-defense, which is what this chapter will cover.

There are many factors to consider when applying selfdefense in real-life situations. First and foremost, avoid risky areas and risky situations. Following are some additional tips to keep in mind.

- The seriousness of the attack will determine the severity of your response. If it is a simple situation among neighbors or friends, you must defend with techniques that will quell the situation. You don't want to inflict serious harm, if possible.

- During street encounters with strangers, do not take any chances. Your first response should be to talk and try to de- escalate the situation. If that fails and the confrontation escalates, be careful. Remember, even if you get tangled up in a simple exchange of blows, you could strike your head on the pavement when falling or the blow could hit a nerve or vital spot.
- When possible, avoid confrontations, even if it's an affront to your pride. Road rage is a good example of this. Today, you never know what an attacker will do or what kind of weapon he will use. Use your head and avoid confrontations if at all possible.
- As a last resort, estimate your attacker and the situation quickly. Consider what your counter will be.

- If it's obvious that you are not physically as strong as your attacker, what counter move will you use? Remember that kicks can sometimes be an equalizer.
- If you must defend yourself or family and you realize the attacker will cause you grave harm, stop at nothing. Using finger attacks to the eyes and face is extremely serious, but it's an option if needed. Also, attack the throat and vital areas. However, these forms of force must only be used if you are in a life-threatening situation.
- Review your body "weapons" frequently and practice karate-style shadowboxing with imaginary attackers under a variety of conditions.
- If you are attacked and see an opportunity to escape, do so.
- Be absolutely sure you are justified in your counterattack. If you have stopped an attacker and continue hitting or kicking him after he is incapacitated, you could be legally responsible as an attacker.

*Chapter 4 — Self-Defense Techniques*

In this section on self-defense techniques, you will apply **TCChniqilCS** blocks, stances, evasions and counterattacks against punches and kicks. You should attack and defend aggressively, but use caution so you do not injure your partner.

Since most attacks come as a surprise, note how the defender stands in photo No.1 of the sequences. You will notice that she stands with her hands at her sides as the

attacker prepares to launch a fist or a leg.

It's imperative that the defender learns to move in all directions while applying the block. Meanwhile, the attacker is learning to deliver punches and kicks at a moving target. This pre-determined attacker/defender method is later accelerated, and your skill level improves. As you learn and develop, both participants should begin to improve their speed and timing. Eventually, you will both reach your maximum.

1 Start all of the techniques as shown. This is *ippon kumite* or one-point sparring.

2 To begin, the attacker steps in deep with a face punch. The defender pulls away from the attack into a forward stance and prepares to counter.

3 Using a palm heel strike, the defender launches a counterattack. Striking under the nose can be dangerous, so alternate targets are the chin and other areas.

**65**

**1** Starting position

**2** The attacker throws a punch to the face or upper body. The defender pulls back and to the outside into a *kibadachi* (horse stance) while using a forearm block.

**3** Compared to the attacker, the defender is in a strong position. She then grasps the extended punching hand and delivers an elbow counter under the armpit.

NOTE: *In the beginning, while learning blocks, stances and other moves, throw just one counter. As soon as possible, however, add multiple counterattacks.*

*Chapter 4 — Self-Defense Techniques*

*1* Starting stance

*2* The attacker steps in and throws a face punch. The defender immediately goes into a back stance while using an inside forearm block.

*3* The defender then counters with forward hand to the face or throat. Notice how she also switches to a forward stance for more power.

*1* Starting position

*2* When the attacker lunges in with an upper-body blow, the defender pulls back at an angle into a back stance and uses a shuto uke (knife-hand block).

*3* The defender switches to a forward stance as she delivers a reverse thrust to the throat.

*1* The fighters square off.

*2* The attacker lunges into a punch attack. The defender, who pulls back at a slight angle into a cat stance, uses an open-hand grab block.

*3* From the cat stance, the defender counters with a front kick to the face. Note: That was not her only target. She also could have gone for the stomach, groin, legs, etc.

*Chapter 4 — Self-Defense Techniques*

**1** The pair square off.

**2** When the attacker steps in with a lunge punch to the face, the defender steps to the outside while using a flat palm parry block. Going to the outside of an attacker's arm is better for the defender because it makes the attacker more vulnerable.

**3** The defender uses her blocking hand to deflect the attacker's arm downward. She then counters with an elbow strike. To close the gap while counter attacking, the defender may need to execute a "shuffle" or "sliding" motion.

*1* The fighters square off.

*2* As the attacker lunges in with a face or body punch, the defender shifts to the outside using a wrist hook block (the back of the hand hooks over the forward arm). You'll notice that she is in a cat stance.

*3* From the outside position, the defender uses her leg and hooks behind the attacker's

knee. The defender sweeps back and upward to throw the attacker. Notice how she also uses her block hand to push backward. Once the attacker has fallen, she can add counters with kicks, etc.

*Chapter 4 — Self-Defense Techniques*

*1* The two square off.

*2* The attacker lunges in and grabs or shoves her opponent with both hands. The defender uses a palm heel block or slight variation and deflects both of the attacker's arms. Then, she counter grabs the attacker.

*3* The defender then can counter with a kick to the groin or a knee if she's in close.

*1* Starting position

*2* The attacker starts with an overhand strike to the head. First, the defender pulls back into a forward stance and uses an upward "X" block.

*3* Next, she counters with a finger thrust to the eyes. Of course, there are other options.

NOTE: *When you use the "X" block on an overhead blow, you can sometimes stop the strike before it starts on its downward path.*

Chapter 4 — Self-Defense Techniques

Your shifting, maneuvers and stances become more important against kicks because of their power.

## Kick Defenses

*1* Starting position

*2* The attacker delivers a front kick to the midsection. The defender shifts outside of the kick and utilizes a forearm block. Notice the defender's position. She is to the side and outside of the attacker.

*3* The defender then counter twists her body back toward the attacker and counters with a ridge hand to the neck.

73

**1** The fighters get ready.

**2** The attacker delivers a front kick, and the defender responds by stepping in with an "X" block. Note: You should only step into the kick if you can stop it before it starts its powerful forward progress. If the kick is moving forward, stepping back may be a better defense.

**3** The defender then counters with an "X" strike to the attacker's throat. In this case, and in all situations, you can visualize many counters that may be used. Use mental exercises and visualize different defenses and counters in all of your practice.

*Chapter 4 — Self-Defense Techniques*

*1* Ready position

*2* When the attacker throws a front kick, the defender pulls back into a forward stance and scoop blocks the kick by grasping under her opponent's leg. The defender also twists her hips to help misdirect the kick so it passes by her body as she executes the block.

*3* The defender attacks her

strike. From this technique, she can also execute a throw ınd and pushing down on the knee with her striking

75

*1* In this instance, the attacker shuffles forward and kicks with her front leg.

*2* As the attacker delivers a sidekick, the defender steps sideways into a forward stance and executes a down block.

*3* As the attacker falls forward, the defender executes a low- side thrust kick to the back of the attacker's knee. The defender could also throw elbows or strikes to the back of the head.

*4* Close-up of the arm position of a down block to the leg.

## Advanced Response Techniques

This section deals with more advanced methods of building your responses for attacks. Now, both the defender and attacker will be in a "ready" or fighting position and defend and attack from here. This is known as *jiyu ippon* kumite or free one-point sparring.

In the prior section of ippon kumite, both students are building basic attack and defense responses. In this level, the attacker delivers blows and kicks from a fighting position. The attacker will also deliver the attacks "deeper" and follow the defender more realistically; therefore, the defender must be more accurate and skillful both in defense and counterattacks. By the way, counterattacks also will be done from a defensive position, so you must learn to strike, or kick, from here.

In basic training, you must train your muscles and reactions in the fundamentals. Now, however, you must train to deliver all of your blows and kicks from a variety of positions. After all, you never know in which situation you may find yourself.

While engaged, maintain focus *(kime),* deep concentration and eye contact with your attacker at all times. You must train yourself to ignore distractions, keep your eyes on your attacker and keep that focus.

As you advance in your training, you will find a comfortable position from which to fight that suits your body type. Even then, it's important to learn a variety of positions so you can meet all challenges.

Because this art includes hand and foot fighting, you must keep a guard from which your hands can defend either hand or foot attacks.

*1* The defender and attacker are in ready or fighting positions.

*2* When the attacker slides forward with a front hand jab, the defender assumes a cat stance and uses a backhand block, deflecting the technique outward as he changes his leg position toward the outside of the attacker.

*3* The defender then slides in under the attacker's arm and uses a counter-downward elbow strike to the armpit. This can be done in a horse stance (kiba dachi) or a sochin stance.

*4* The defender then turns his hips so he's in a forward stance and throws an elbow to the face.

*Chapter 4 — Self-Defense Techniques*

*1* Starting position

*2* The attacker slides in with a front punch. The defender withdraws slightly and uses a forearm block, turning the attacker inward.

*3* Using strong hip movements, the defender throws a backhand chop over the attacker's arm, striking the neck or the face.

*4* The defender uses an instep kick to the back of the attacker's knee, driving him to the floor.

*5* The defender, using lots of hip action, throws a vicious elbow to the attacker's head. Notice that he is also in a forward stance.

*1* Starting position

*2* The attacker slides into a face punch. In response, the defender shifts back slightly and uses a combination "X" block and backhand block.

*3* The defender then grasps the attacker's extended arm and pulls him in as he delivers a hammer fist backhand to the chest.

*4* Still gripping the attacker's arm, the defender raises his arm and prepares to strike downward.

*5* The defender completes the technique with an elbow break of the attacker's arm.

*Chapter 4 — Self-Defense Techniques*

*1* Starting position

*2* When the attacker slides deep into a forward stance and delivers a body punch, the defender pulls back at an angle, defending with a downward knifehand block.

*3* The defender twists his hips toward the attacker and delivers a front kick.

*4* The defender drops into a forward stance and strikes an uppercut.

**81**

*1* Starting position

*2* The attacker lunges with a front punch, forcing the defender to slide back and outside of the attacker's front foot. As he grasps the attacker's arm, the defender uses his front leg to hook behind the attacker's knee to pull and break his balance.

*3* The defender twists the attacker to a vulnerable position and raises his free hand so he's ready to deliver a backhand blow.

*4* The defender delivers the backhand to the face or neck.

*Chapter 4 — Self-Defense Techniques*

*1* The defender assumes a cat stance.

*2* The attacker begins a forward punch attack. The defender anticipates this and moves back and to the side, delivering a side thrust kick.

*3* The defender then drops his kicking leg so he is now in a forward stance, he closes the distance and delivers an upward strike to the chin.

*1* The fighters square off.

*2* The defender can counter with a front leg front kick.

*3* As the defender drops his kicking leg into a forward position, he latches onto his opponent's throat with a claw grab.

*4* Demonstrating strong hip action, the defender follows up with an inside ridge hand to the neck, jaw, etc.

The following section deals with sacrifice kicks. The photos depict the defender applying various kicks from the ground. Therefore, you should practice dropping down and throwing your kicks at the attacker standing over you.

Some might wonder why it's necessary to kick from the ground. The reality is that you may slip and fall, get knocked down or be overwhelmed by an attacker's forward momentum. Thus, you have to be prepared.

From the ground, you can apply front kicks, side kicks and sometimes even back kicks. The available targets from this position include the attacker's ankles, knees, calves, thighs, groin and lower body.

Of course, if you find yourself on the ground accidentally, get up as quickly as possible so you can defend yourself from your feet. To be sure, fighting on the ground will limit your counters. Therefore, you should only fight on the ground when you are forced to. Under all circumstances, you want to stand up as quickly as you can.

## Throwing to the Ground

1 Start from any position.

2 When you're defending against a kick, it's vitally important to shift your body with the block. Here, the defender has shifted outside and used a grab block on his attacker's leg. Notice how he has scooped under the kicker's leg.

3 Next, the defender smashes down on the attacker's leg with an elbow blow.

4 Still grasping the leg, he grasps some clothing or can throw the attacker off balance by coming up under the neck.

*Chapter 4 — Self-Defense Techniques*

5 The defender can now lift the leg and throw the attacker to the ground.

6 Once the attacker is on the ground, he may apply any counter, strike or kick.

*1* Starting position

*2* The attacker throws a side or roundhouse kick. The defender shifts to the outside, uses a grasp block under the attacker's leg and prepares to counter.

*3* He then throws a backhand or chop action to the head, neck, etc.

*4* The defender shifts his leg so that it is inside the attacker's. While firmly grasping the attacker's leg and grabbing his clothing or shoulder, he prepares to throw him.

*Chapter 4 — Self-Defense Techniques*

5 The defender then pulls his leg against the attacker's, throwing him to the ground. You should control your attacker all the way to the ground, provided he is your practice partner. If you're on the street, smash him hard into the ground.

6 Once he's on the ground, keep control of him so you can deliver any number of counters, blows to the groin, kicks, etc.

## Chapter 5

# Throws and Sweeps

Throwing, sweeping and takedowns are techniques found in the martial arts of judo, jujutsu and aikido, among others. During karate's early growth, many of its students also had a foundation in judo and jujutsu. You could see the influence of the other arts when the students executed throws and sweeps.

As time went on, karate began to attract participants from the other arts and from the general population. Gradually, throwing and sweeps became used less and less. Nevertheless, karate always had a foundation of sweeps, takedowns and throws that remain inherent to the art. And so it is today.

Learning the many ways of judo and jujutsu requires years of hard, arduous training, so this is not the objective in this section. Rather, we will give you some of the quick and simple — but effective — ways to bring an opponent down.

Remember, this is generally stand-up, hand-and-foot fighting, but you must know some of the rudiments of throws and sweeps.

Most importantly, techniques must be applied when the opportunity presents itself. For example, if you are determined to throw an opponent at all costs, you may be hit or kicked in the process.

Every technique you learn — whether its hitting, kicking, throwing or sweeping — must only be applied when you see an opening ... when the opportunity is there.

Also, in the world of real combat during the turbulent war years of Japan, the motive behind a throw was to smash your attacker into the ground — head first — if possible. You wanted to cause the most serious injury possible, taking him out of the battle.

Today, we learn to fall properly so we can practice freely with a partner without injury. Therefore, in practice, control your partner to the ground. If you find yourself in a street selfdefense situation, use your judgment as to how you want him to land.

*IMPORTANT: On forward throws, leverage and balance are more effective and important against opponents who are taller or the same size. Opponents who are shorter or stockier make forward throws more difficult.*

## Hip Throw
## Uki Goshi

1 This is an *uki goshi* (hip throw). As the attacker prepares to strike with a punch, the defender steps in, jams the attacker and prepares to grab his punching arm.

2 The defender then wraps his other arm around his opponent's waist, grabbing his belt, if possible.

Chapter 5 — Throws and Sweeps

3 When you execute this throw, your body should now be facing the same direction as the attacker's. Next, bend your knees, thrust your hips hard into his pelvis and lift. To lift your opponent completely off the ground, you'll really need your legs and hips.

4 Thrust your hips upward, using leg strength. Meanwhile, while you pull on his one arm that you've secured, pull with your other arm that is around his waist and twist.

5 Your opponent is now completely off balance, in the air and defenseless.

6 The throw is now complete. You can counter attack with blows and kicks or you can pin him to the ground.

**IMPORTANT:** *Deliberately turning your back to an attacker is wrong. However, there will be times, such as when you are close-in fighting, in which you find yourself jammed in. In that case, you may have no alternative.*

The key to the hip throw is to lift your opponent off the floor, using your legs and hips. Practice this lifting technique many times until you can lift even heavy opponents off the ground.

## Shoulder Throw
### Seionage

The principles of the shoulder throw are much like the hip throw. They are best used for close-in situations and/or when your attacker is behind you or grabbing from behind.

Our illustration demonstrates a defense technique from the front, simply because you must know the proper way to execute a shoulder throw.

As with the hip throw, step in and jam your attacker. Keep your feet close together for balance. Bend at the knees and keep your back as straight as possible. When one arm defends, the other is free to counter strike.

1 The attacker raises his arm to strike.

2 As Dan Ivan illustrates, you step in and block with one hand while your other hand reaches under his arm.

3 As you grasp his wrist or forearm, your other hand wraps around his arm, clasping his shoulder tight to you. Next, prepare to lift with your entire body.

*Chapter 5 — Throws and Sweeps*

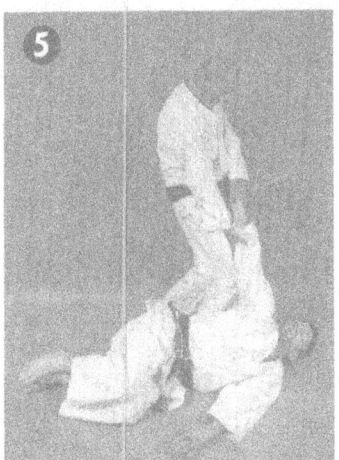

NOTE: *In all forward throws, do not leave space between your body and the attacker. Space gives him leverage, so you want to stay tight.*

4 Lift with your legs and hips and pull with both arms. Bend your body forward so that you lift him off the ground, wrapped over your back and defenseless.

5 Drop your attacker to the ground and follow-up with whatever you would like to end the fight.

NOTE: *In some instances, you may even drop forward to your knee to accomplish this throw.*

## Legbar Throw
Taiotoshi

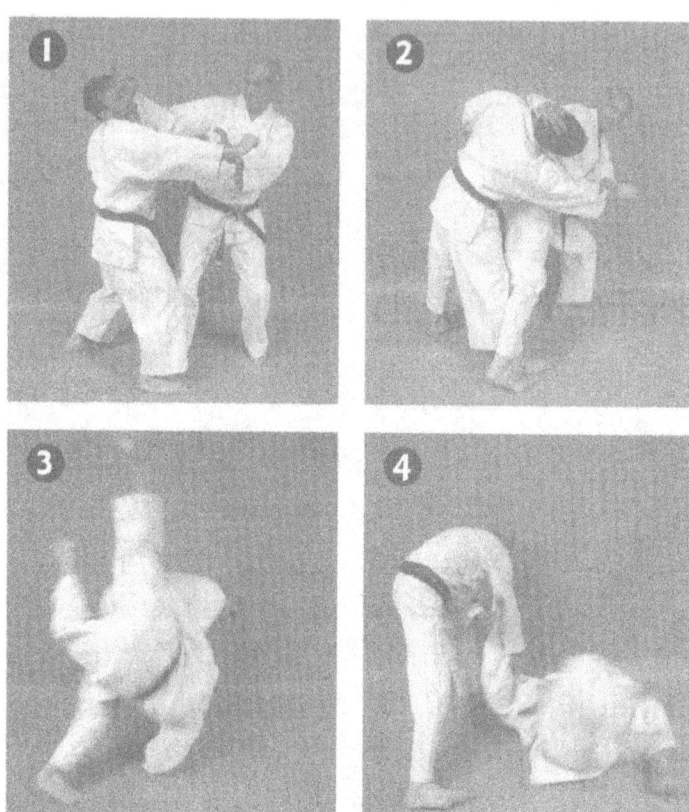

*1* This is a version of the *taiotoshi* throw.

*2* The defender blocks the attacker's leg as illustrated and grasps his head and arm.

*3* The defender then pulls on his attacker's arm and head while twisting him into the throw.

*4* The defender follows up with a strike or submission hold.

*Chapter 5 — Throws and Sweeps*

# Leg Hook Osotogari

1 This technique is an *osotogari* (leg hook), which can be categorized as a throw or a trip. To begin, the attacker prepares to step in with a face attack.

2 The defender side steps, blocks and delivers a counter blow to the attacker. A quick counter blow can hurt an attacker or distract him to set up the throw.

3 The defender then jams in deep so he can hook his leg behind the attacker's and breaks his balance backward.

4 With the power of your leg, pull back hard and push the attacker, leaning into the throw.

5 Complete the throw by lifting your leg and smashing your attacker to the ground.

*se the gap between you and your opponent, g him backward. Your balance should be id you are leaning backward instead of into*

## Sweep
## Ashi Barai

*Ashi barai* is the term applied to sweeps. There are many versions, but, for brevity, we will term them all as ashi barai.

**1** The attacker slides in with his forward leg to deliver a blow.

**2** The defender blocks the technique and grasps the attacker's arm. This is a close-in position.

**3** The defender then breaks the attacker's balance backward, steps in between his legs and hooks him behind his knee (you can also hook your foot behind his heel).

**4** The defender then sweeps back his leg and pushes the opponent backward with both hands.

**5** As the attacker hits the ground, you can follow up with a kick. When the attacker hits the ground, be careful that his leg doesn't fly up and kick you.

*Chapter 5 — Throws and Sweeps*

*1* The attacker slides in with his forward leg to deliver a blow.

*2* The defender blocks the strike and "catches" the attacker's forward leg with the insole of his foot. If the timing is good, the defender will sweep the instant the attacker's foot touches the ground.

*3* The defender twists his hips and sweeps the attacker's leg as he pulls his arm.

*4* As the attacker falls forward, the defender reverses his stance into a strong forward position and strikes his opponent as he is falling.

*1* As the attacker moves in to deliver a blow, the defender also prepares to move in.

*2* The defender slides to the outside, slightly behind the attacker, as he blocks the strike. The defender throws his other arm across his attacker's body. To break his attacker's balance, he aims high under the head.

*3* He then twists his body and uses his arm to throw his attacker over his leg.

*4* As the attacker drops to the floor, he can deliver the proper counter blow or kick.

*5* This is a back view of how you position your leg behind the attacker to prevent him from evading the throw.

*Chapter 5 — Throws and Sweeps*

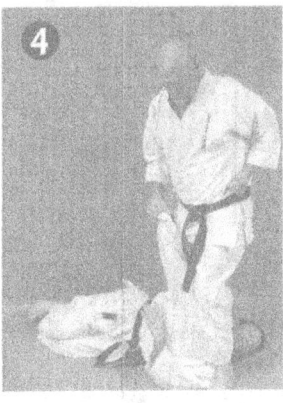

1 This sweep is one of the most common used in karate. The goal is to catch your attacker's foot from the outside as he steps in.

2 Timing is essential. You may even be the aggressor for this sweep and catch your attacker's forward foot as illustrated.

3 Using your hips, pull your attacker hard as you sweep his legs-

4 Once your attacker is on the ground, you may use a submission armbar technique or follow up with a blow or kick.

In karate training, sweeps are more prevalent than throws. When executing a sweep, timing is very important. Your objective is to catch your opponent's foot or leg at the moment he moves. If he is standing solid, with all of his weight on the leg you wish to sweep, it will be more difficult.

# Chapter 6

# Defenses Against Grabs and Holds

In this section, you'll get a good idea of just how broad karate really is. Among other topics, we'll discuss the numerous ways that an attacker may confront you. Things like grabbing, holding and restraining. These are the types of things you things you're about to learn how to do.

Basic karate improves your striking and kicking skills. You also learn to develop power and speed. However, those aren't the only elements that comprise karate training. You also have defensive maneuvers such as blocking and footwork, both of which are also important.

However, this section deals with holds and grabs, common ways in which a confrontation typically starts. You will also learn techniques labeled judo, aikido, and jujutsu. But all are part of a thorough course in Japanese karate, as it was taught in its original form.

While many of these techniques are lost to the modern day karate instructor, that doesn't mean they are not valuable. To the contrary, they should be included as part of a comprehensive Japanese karate training program.

When training, start slow and learn where your "balance" points are. Eventually, throw

*1* Your opponent steps up and grabs your wrist.

*2* In response, you may throw a counter kick to his knee (or groin).

*3* Pull your arm away in a semi-circle. You are working at his weakest point of his grip ... his thumb and fingers.

*4* Pull your hand free and grasp (see photo A).

*5* Twist his hand and throw him. Remember to put your hip and body into the throw. For better balance, go into a forward stance.

*6* Follow up with a kick. Of course, you could always go with an elbow or wrist pressure.

*Chapter 6 — Defenses Against Grabs and Holds*

*A* This photo has been reversed

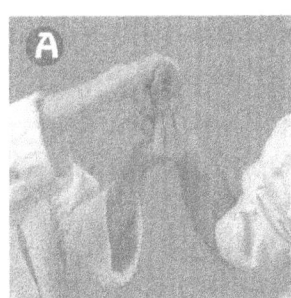

1 Using both hands, the opponent grabs the wrist.

2 The defender counters with a knee kick to the groin. She also has a free hand with which to strike.

3 She steps in and grabs her hand.

4 She then strikes her opponent under the chin with her elbow. Notice how she uses both of her leverage. The knee to the groin is the 1e hold and then she can wrap up the 1e chin.

**105**

*1* Your opponent grabs your wrist with his opposite hand.

*2* You can then counter with a front kick. At the same time, twist your hand and grab his wrist.

*3* Lock his hand to yours with your free hand. Now you have a two-hand grip on his wrist and hand.

*4* Keep his elbow bent and twist inward and down on his wrist.

*5* A kick to the rib cage will disable your opponent.

**NOTE:** *When done properly, you will apply pressure to your opponent's wrist. That's why it's imperative that you maintain a strong grip, keep his elbow bent, and twist inward and down.*

*Chapter 6 — Defenses Against Grabs and Holds*

1 Your opponent grabs your lapels with both hands.

2 You counter with a knee to the groin.

3 Grab his wrists and hands with both of your own hands.

4 Using leverage against his wrist, twist and throw. Use your own body leverage, keeping his hand close to you for better control.

5 When your opponent is down, you can do a number of things, including applying wrist and elbow pressure, throwing a kick or holding him down as a restraint.

1 The opponent grabs with a headlock.

2 Strike his groin with a punch or ridge hand chop.

3 Using your free hand, push upward at his chin. For better results, push at the tip of his nose.

4 Set up for a throw by grabbing behind his knee and lift as you push with your other hand.

5 While your opponent is on the ground, you can throw a variety of counters, including strikes, kicks or some of the submission techniques. (From a headlock, you can also bite your opponent to free yourself from a hold.)

NOTE: *In most instances, when your opponent holds or grabs you, your arms and legs are free. That's when it's time for a* quick and decisive counter. In your arsenal, you should have kicks, punches and throws. Use your imagination when practicing with a friendly opponent and practice different options.

**1** The opponent attacks by grabbing the throat.

**2** You can counter with an upward strike to the nose, chin or eyes. Don't neglect the knee to the groin. That's another good technique when an attacker is in front of you.

**3** Continue your counterattack by using your other hand to claw at his face. Prepare to turn your body and break the hold by bringing your arms over his.

**4** Step through and across your opponents' body, bring your arm around and throw a backhand elbow to his face.

NOTE: *Realistically, gouging at the face and eyes may be enough to thwart an attacker. However, we have included more possibilities and techniques so that you can train for a variety of responses.*

*1* Your opponent attacks from behind and grabs your neck and shoulders.

*2* Counter by striking his groin with a backhand chop.

*3* Raise your arm up and over his.

*4* You can lock up both of his arms by holding them tight to your body. Notice the footwork. To get in the proper position to counter, you must constantly move so you are in a better position.

*5* There are a number of counter strikes you can throw from this position, including a ridge hand, a reverse punch to the rib cage, an elbow blow to the ribs, or even a roundhouse knee to the ribs.

*Chapter 6 — Defenses Against Grabs and Holds*

**1** Your opponent grabs you from behind in a bear hug, locking your arms.

**2** You can counter by bending forward, creating a bit of space between you and your opponent. While you are doing this, bring your leg up and get ready to kick.

**3** Stomp down hard with your heel on his instep or ankle. This will help to break his hold.

**4** Grab his arm and begin a shoulder throw. Remember, keep his body close to you, begin to pull and twist.

**5** Complete the throw as illustrated. From this position, you can execute a shoulder and hip throw.

**NOTE:** *When you have a grip on an opponent, keep twisting and pulling toward the ground. In some instances, you may drop to one knee for better leverage.*

1 Your opponent grabs both of your wrists from behind.

2 First, counter with a back kick to the groin. If you are in close, bring your heel up and kick. If you are further back, a straight back kick will do.

3 Throw your arms up and slide back to the outside of your opponent.

4 As you position yourself, grab his wrist with one hand and his elbow with your other hand. Now you are set up for some leverage.

*Chapter 6 — Defenses Against Grabs and Holds*

5 Begin stepping in, pushing on your opponent's elbow to force him down.

6 Maintain a strong grip and control your opponent until he is face down.

7 In this example, the defender steps across the opponent's arm and now has control by elbow pressure. You may use any variety of counters, kicks, strikes, etc.

*1* Your opponent attacks from the rear, either grabbing your clothing or your hair.

*2* Pivot to one side and throw a groin strike.

*3* Next, pivot into a solid stance and continue your attack with your other hand to his groin.

*4* Grab your opponent's ankle and put pressure on his knee.

*Chapter 6 — Defenses Against Grabs and Holds*

5 Pull upward on his ankle and push down and back on his knee to throw him.

6 Many openings now present themselves for a finishing technique, including a kick, strike, etc.

*NOTE: In prior sections, we mentioned that techniques are interchangeable. You may respond with only strikes and kicks or you can mix in some throws. The situation will always determine what is the appropriate response.*

# Chapter 7

# Chokes and Submission Holds

Karate is a striking art, so chokeholds and ground fighting are secondary. However, these techniques are in here, and you should know them. Incidentally, we believe that striking and hitting techniques are quicker and easier to learn for the average person than the grappling arts. If you do have some trouble with them, have some patience. You will get it. Furthermore, for the purpose of this text, we will offer techniques that are simple and easy for a novice to learn.

In the past, a well-rounded course in karate included chokes, leverage and pressure techniques. However, things changed a little bit because of the emphasis on sport karate. As a result, many schools teach very little, if any, of the above techniques in these modern times. On the other hand, we (the authors) do cover ground arts more extensively in the dojo.

The two primary chokes, of which there are many variations, are the trachea choke and the carotid artery choke. The trachea choke cuts off the air supply through the windpipe. The carotid artery choke shuts down the blood vessels in your neck that carry the blood supply to the brain. In an emergency or explosive street encounter, the trachea choke will possibly be the most natural for you to apply.

You must exercise extreme caution when you execute any choke. If you apply too much pressure, trachea chokes can crush the windpipe, which can cause severe damage or even death. Drill this into your brain and act accordingly.

During practice with a friendly partner, both of you must learn the significance of "tapping." Some of you may be unfamiliar with this term. When the pressure of the choke becomes too severe, you tap your hand or foot on your opponent or on the floor. This means your partner must immediately release his hold.

We have also concentrated on just one submission technique. In the self-defense section, you will find other pressure and leverage techniques that will cause an opponent to submit.

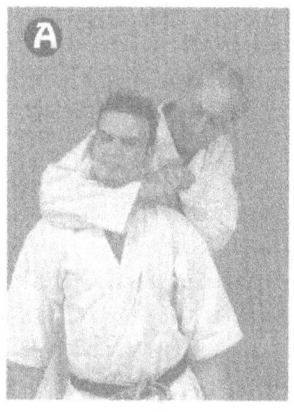

*A* In many confrontations and skirmishes, you could end up grappling while standing or on the ground. So, be prepared. As we mentioned, it's not unusual for your adversary to try to choke you. Front chokes, rear chokes and even headlocks are techniques that are used frequently.

If you're on the ground, you will have more power and leverage if you wrap your legs around your opponent, both from the front and rear.

We do advise that you do what you know best and fight back. However, we will teach you one choke that is quite effective. Remember, as we mentioned previously, every thing you apply should be done when the circumstances are right. Don't struggle for a choke when something like a headbutt or elbow smash is more appropriate.

Chapter 7 — Chokes and Submission Holds

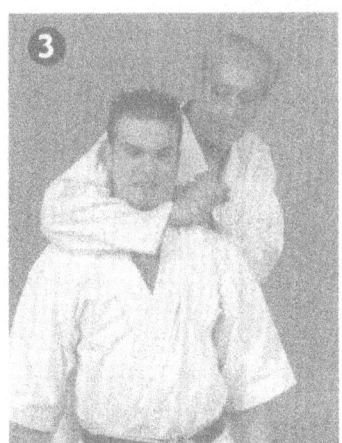

*1* Dan Ivan demonstrates a trachea choke. From the rear, reach around your opponent's neck.

*2* Clasp your hand as shown and situate the bone of your forearm across your opponent's windpipe. Your biceps/upper arm should press against the back of your opponent's head and neck.

*3* With your arm now acting as a vice, apply pressure against the windpipe. This is quick and effective, but it's also extremely dangerous.

Therefore, use caution. While practicing with a friend, apply light and slow pressure until you learn the technique. Don't forget to tap when the pressure becomes too great.

**119**

1 The trachea choke may be applied while standing, lying or kneeling. In this instance, instead of clasping the hand to apply pressure, one hand will fit under the arm. While grappling, there are occasions when this opening will present itself. Next, grasp the clothing and pull down tightly. You need this as leverage.

2 Encircle his neck with your other arm and hold your forearm against his throat. Your upper arm and shoulder form the "vice."

3 Grab his shoulder as illustrated. If possible, grab your opponent's clothing. You need a strong grip for the leverage and pressure. Hold tightly with your other arm while pulling down for better control.

*Chapter 7 — Chokes and Submission Holds*

This is the same choke shown from the front. Again, this choke can be applied if you are mounted on top of your opponent, standing or kneeling. If you are standing, try to push your opponent against a wall because this will give you better leverage.

1 Cross grab at his clothing and pull him toward you.

2 Grab his clothing and wedge your fingers under his lapel or collar. Hold tight for control.

3 Thrust your forearm against his throat. Pull down hard with your other hand and apply pressure against your opponent's neck.

NOTE: *In karate, this is often used as a forearm smash to the throat.*

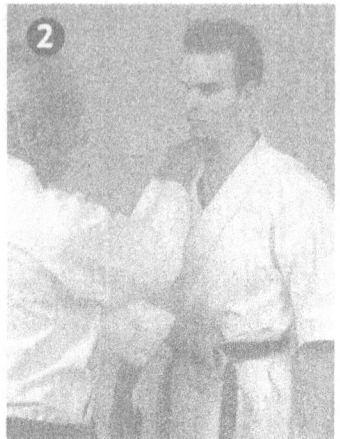

This choke is similar to the trachea choke on the prior page. This time you will learn to do the choke without relying on your opponent's clothing-

1 To begin, your "control" hand grabs at your opponent's belt or the inside of his trousers.

2 Reach up and grasp his shoulder with your other hand. Hold tightly with both hands for control.

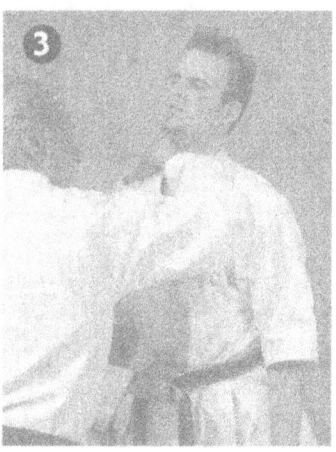

3 Apply pressure against his throat with your forearm.

NOTE: *This choke is strongest when you are mounted on top of your opponent. For more control when you're on the ground, wrap your legs around your opponent.*

*Chapter 7 — Chokes and Submission Holds*

 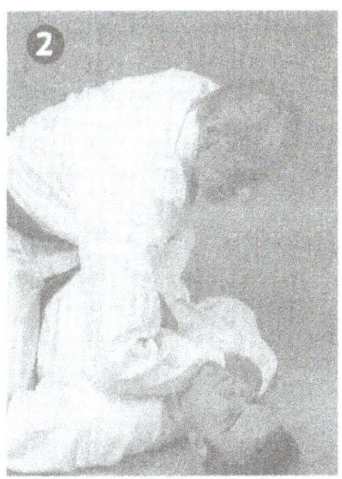

These photos illustrate how much more pressure and leverage you will have when mounted on top of your opponent.

## Submissions

One of the most often used submission techniques, especially when you are on the ground, is the armbar. You can render an opponent helpless by applying pressure to the elbow joint. Variations of this technique are illustrated in the following photographs.

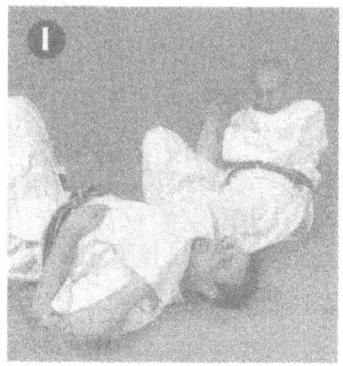

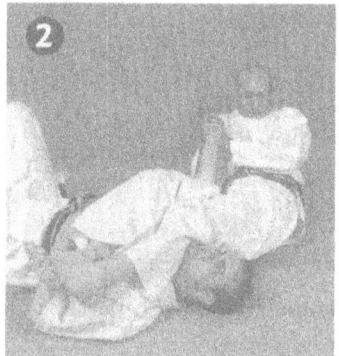

1 Taking your opponent down is discussed in other parts of this text. Therefore, we won't cover that here. Instead, we'll concentrate just on the armbar.

To begin, place one of your legs over the neck/throat of your opponent while you pull his arm toward you. Place his elbow across your inner thigh. Grasp his hand firmly (make sure you are working against the joint) and pull down until he submits. Your other leg should be jammed against his body.

2 This is essentially the same technique, except now both of your legs are across his body. This provides better control.

Squeeze his arm between your legs as you apply pressure downward against his elbow.

**3** This is the same armbar, but the control is different. One of your legs is high, tight against his armpit. Spread your other leg out for better balance. Reach around his neck and press down with your chest against him. You already have a hold of his wrist. Now apply elbow pressure by pressing down.

Wrist pressure or leverage, which is used in many of the martial arts, is another common way to apply a submission hold. We have included four variations of the wrist lock.

Armbars and wrist locks are used frequently because you have control of your opponent's arms when you execute most of your throws, trips and sweeps.

"PEACE, SKY, EARTH, PEOPLE, MOON, KNOWLEDGE, DO"

*Hironoshi Ohtsuka*

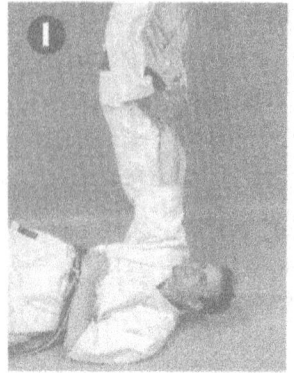

1 While grasping your opponent's hand, you may apply pressure on the wrist. Your leg should simultaneously apply pressure to the elbow joint.

2 This provides a closer look at the proper way to grasp the hand to apply the wrist lock. Notice how the leg is situated differently from the other position.

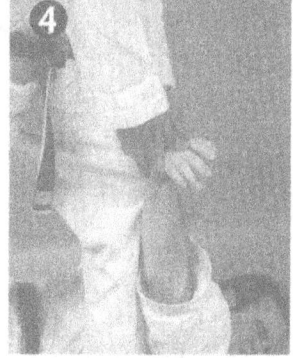

3 In this photograph, you can see that there is a similar pressure against both the wrist and elbow. However, now you have rolled your opponent onto his stomach for better control. You may also drop one knee on his back

4 A close up to better see the proper wrist and elbow pressure.

*NOTE: Submission techniques evolved from the*

Some of you may be wondering why you would apply a submission hold. Good question. If you are in a confrontation with a stranger, you must evaluate the situation. Are you in grave danger? Is your attacker physically bigger and stronger than you are? Is a striking technique to the vital targets a better way to defend?

After considering all of the above questions, following are some options:

- Use a submission hold if it's a non-serious situation. This might be an angry friend or neighbor, etc. In this situation, perhaps a submission hold will calm him down. This can be a good way to defuse the situation.
- Remember, you have no referee, no judge and no one to declare you a winner. Therefore, think of what you are trying to achieve, and a submission hold might just be appropriate.

# Chapter 8

# ground Fighting

In this section, we have included specific techniques to help you fight while you are on the ground. However, as in the previous chapter, we are going to keep the techniques simple and easy to learn. And, of course, these techniques are effective.

While you (a karate student) are engaged in ground fighting, you should continue to apply what you have learned, including hitting, kicking, clawing, gouging, using your knees and head-butting. You can apply all of this while you are going down, on the ground, while rolling around and while grappling on the ground.

If you have had extensive training in judo, jujutsu or other grappling arts, then you have other options/techniques, too. For the karate student, however, you should stick to what you know best.

While you should learn how to handle yourself on the ground, get to your feet as fast as possible. Fighting on your feet is your forte. An attacker may kick you while you're down, so you should roll away from him and rise up as quickly as possible. Sometimes you can roll into your opponent's legs and knock him down. Then you can quickly get to your feet.

1 The opponents face each other.

2 The opponent dives in to grab your legs.

3 You counter by grasping his head with both of your hands. Using leverage, twist his head to throw your opponent. Watch your balance, turn and kneel to maintain control.

4 Flip your opponent over onto his back. From this vulnerable position, you may counter with strikes or kicks. There are other options, too. You could use a submission technique against his elbow/arm.

NOTE: *You can also slap both of your palms against your attacker's ears, throw a knee to his face, a chop to his neck or a punch to his face.*

*Chapter 8 — Ground Fighting*

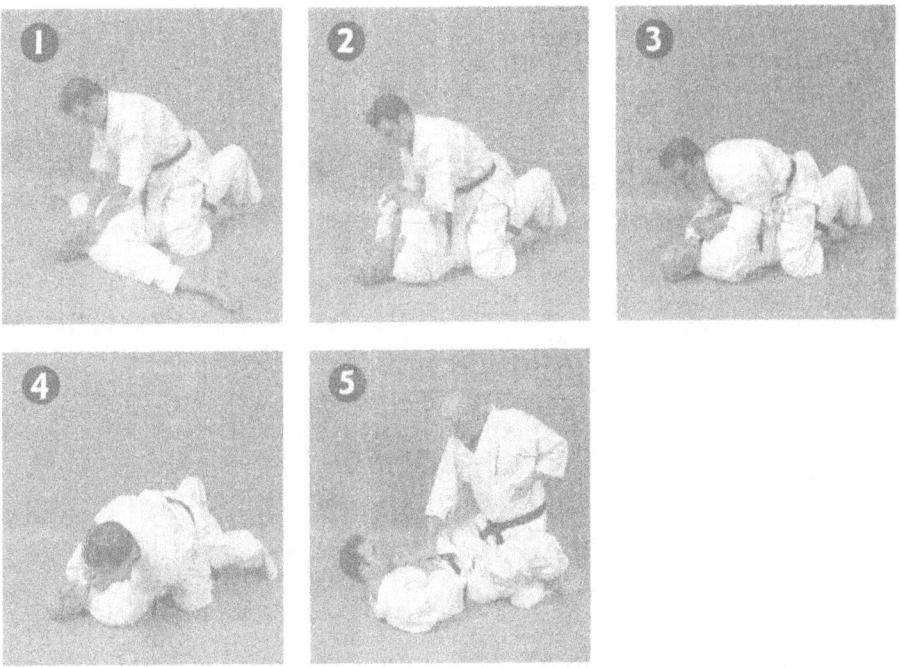

**1** You are on your back, an opponent mounts you and starts choking you.

**2** Reach across his arms and press down. Grab his opposite arm with both hands. Lock his hand down and reach behind his elbow. Bridge your body to help get your opponent off balance.

**3** Twist your body, push at his elbow and use your leg to lift.

**4** You'll be able to upset him with a combination of body torque, pressure against his elbow and lifting your leg. This will upset him, turn him over and you will be on top.

**5** From this control position, you can finish the altercation with strikes or restraining chokes covered in other sections.

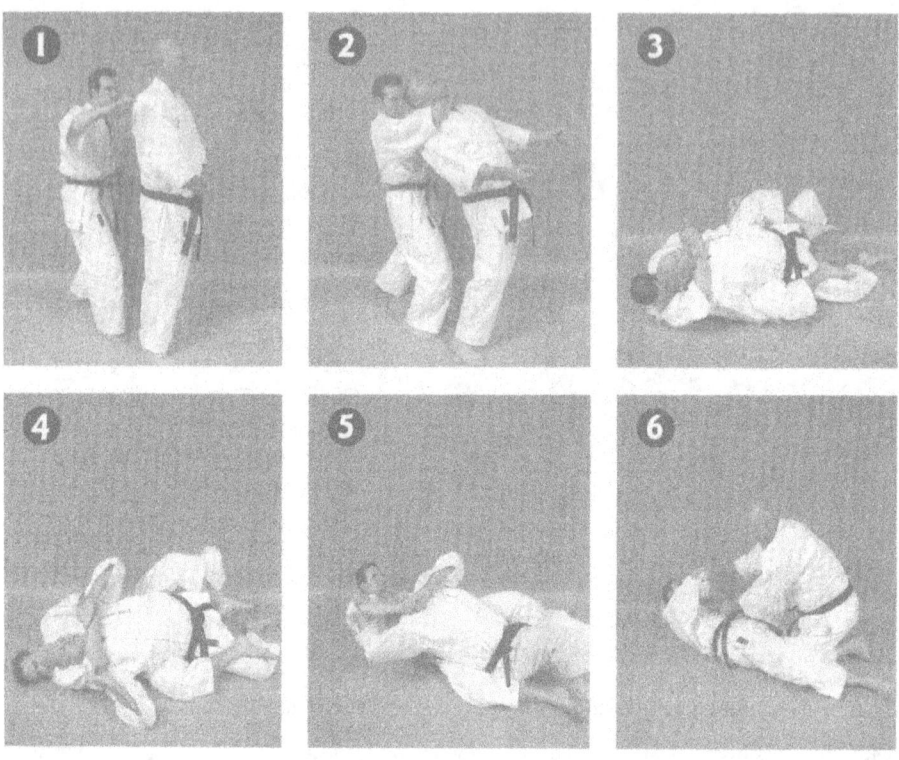

*1* The opponent approaches from the rear to attack.

*2* He pulls you down by grabbing your head/neck.

*3* Your opponent holds you by the neck and wraps his legs around your torso.

*4* To relieve pressure on your neck, pull down on his arm on one side and push upward on his elbow with your other arm.

*5* While pushing up on his elbow, turn your body over and pull down and out.

*6* You can now mount your opponent and counter attack with strikes, kicks, chokes, etc.

*Chapter 8 — Ground Fighting*

1 Your opponent approaches while you are on the ground.

2 Grab his ankles while head-butting his groin. Pull hard on his ankles so you knock him onto his back.

3 You have control, but you must instantly counter with strikes, kicks, etc.

1 Paul Godshaw (kneeling) demonstrates how to deal with an attacker who approaches you from behind while you are on the floor.

2 First, evade by moving forward so you are out of range of an attack. Next, brace yourself on the floor.

3 Counter with a back kick to any exposed target (groin, knee or stomach).

Each photo on these pages illustrates some examples of kicks you can apply from the floor.

Trips, kicks and takedowns should be practiced from the ground position. You can attack your opponent's legs, shins, knees, stomach, groin, etc. Go after whatever is appropriate.

*1* Paul Godshaw demonstrates how to throw kicks from the ground. To begin, his opponent approaches.

*2* Next, he grabs his adversary's gi with his right hand, leans back and fires a kick to the inside of his opponent's right knee..

*Chapter 8 — Ground Fighting*

Always remember that an opponent may approach you and throw a kick or punch. Therefore, drop away from the attack and use your legs for defense.

On all ground techniques, fight and defend until you can quickly get back on your feet.

*1* In this sequence, Paul Godshaw shows a few more kicks from the ground. He throws a shot to the groin.

*2* While holding onto his opponent's gi, Godshaw hammers the side of his knee.

*3* In this technique, Godshaw secures his opponent's left leg with his right leg and drills the inside of the knee.

**135**

# Chapter 9

Whether you're giving it everything you have in a tournament, in class or on the street, you must be aware that falling is inevitable, regardless of how athletic you are. Things happen. Thus, that is the point of this chapter. We're going to teach you how to fall safely so you can get back up and keep training, sparring and/or fighting. The most dangerous part to falling is hitting your head.

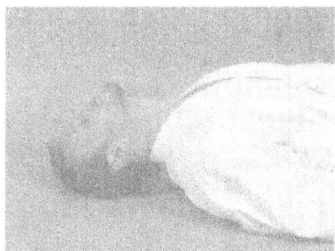

# *Proper Falls to Prevent Injuries*

On a backfall, you must learn how to properly protect your head. To do so, it's vital that you learn how to absorb the fall on your arms.

*1* To begin, stand with your feet about six inches apart, and hold your arms straight in front of you.

*2* Bend at the knees and drop down, so you are in a squat.

Although it is a natural instinct, do not reach for the floor. On

**137**

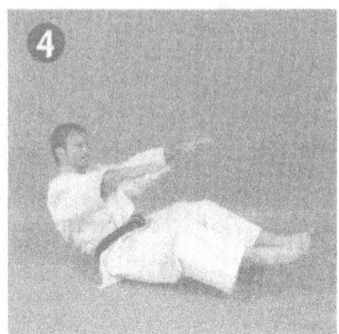

a fast hardback fall, you can injure your wrist or hand by reaching down. Sometimes it's instinctive to catch yourself on your elbow, which is also damaging.

3 Complete the drop and sit on the ground. At first, work on these different stages slowly. Eventually, build some speed so you can learn to fall realistically.

4 Your feet will rise off the floor as your back begins to touch.

5 Tuck your chin to your chest so your head doesn't snap backward on the ground. Absorb or cushion the fall by slapping the entire length of your arms against the ground. It may sting, but it's better than cracking the back of your head on the ground. Your arms act as shock absorbers, along with the surface of your back and shoulders. You might also hit the area between the shoulder blades hard, and that could knock the wind out of you. But, it's certainly better than hitting your head. Besides, with a little training, your arms will take the brunt of the fall.

*Chapter 9 — Proper Falls to Prevent Injuries*

This lesson on falling, along with the other methods, applies to sudden, forceful falls that could result in injury. Falling forward could mean smashing your face into the pavement or damaging your hands and wrists by trying to catch yourself. To prevent this, you want to absorb the fall with your forearms and hands flat.

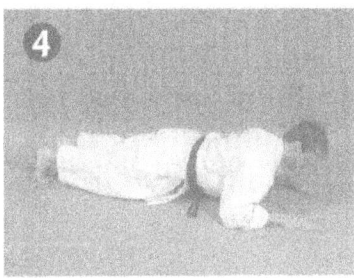

*1* Begin standing with your feet about one foot apart and your arms in front of your chest, perpendicular to your body.

*2 and 3* Start falling forward, making sure your arms are prepared.

*4* Complete the fall. Make sure you keep your head back and use your entire forearms and hands to keep your body from smashing hard into the ground. In a secondary motion, your body may hit the ground, but your arms will absorb the shock first.

**139**

*1 and 2* Beginners may practice the forward fall first from a kneeling position. Gradually, you can rise up until you can do it from an upright position.

These are side falls and often occur when your opponent sweeps one leg. The principle is somewhat similar to the other falls. Thus, you must protect your head and absorb the fall on your arm, not your hands.

1 To begin, stand with your feet about a foot apart and your hands at your sides, slightly in front.

2 Raise one leg up and across your body.

3 In training, you may lower yourself down. Eventually, however, you should freefall to land on your side.

4 Complete the fall with your chin tucked to your chest and your head away from the ground. Your arms should absorb the shock of the fall. Practice on both sides.

This is a forward roll. It will come in handy if you are tripped or thrown in practice. All you do is learn to protect your head and roll. This fall is not unlike a simple somersault that you may have learned when you were younger. Actually, a somersault is not improper as long as you use your hand and arm to protect your head as you go over.

1 A one-hand roll is used in the martial arts because you never know when your opponent may throw you with one of your own arms. In that case, you have only one free arm to accomplish this fall. Now, you'll be prepared.

2 As you move into the roll, your one hand should be touching the ground to protect your head. As shown, you can also use your other hand to help. Ultimately, however, you should be able to execute this roll with only one hand.

3 When completed, you will end up in a position similar to what you were in following the side throw. Your head should not be touching the ground and your arm should absorb the shock.

*Chapter 9 — Proper Falls to Prevent Injuries*

*4 and 5* These show the same fall from different angles. This should allow you to better understand this fall.

Accomplished martial artists can complete this roll and come up on their feet. In the beginning, start slow. If necessary, use a somersault until you become more familiar with the technique.

# Chapter 10

## *Stretches and Exercises for Mobility, Strength and Health*

As you are well aware, many people live a sedentary life that centers around TV, automobiles, elevators and many other automated mechanical devices designed to make our existence easier. Granted, they may make your life easier, but that is not can to exert yourself physically and to help build or maintain a healthy body. Exercise is good for you and you should get as much as your schedule allows. And by all means, get a physical before you begin a rigorous training routine.

When you strengthen your muscles, you'll improve your coordination, agility and skill. When you select these exercises, make sure you do some cardiovascular exercises that help build a strong and healthy heart.

There certainly are a few exercises out there that fit the criteria, but we have a special recommendation for you. And that is karate. This sport not only improves your heart rate, it enhances your muscles, skill and coordination. On top of that, it is always quite challenging.

Besides giving you a good physical work out, karate also provides mental stimulation. That is an added bonus that to your senior years.

In the next several pages, we will offer a few of the karate exercises we recommend. Most of them deal with stretching, which many in modern medicine are now recognizing as a vital key to keeping the elasticity of your muscles and mobility in your body

Before we begin, following are a few tips that should help you get the most out of your workout:

- Get your blood circulating first. Jump up and down for a few minutes until you are warm. Perhaps you can do some jumping jacks.
- While standing, raise your arms up into the air and twist and turn to loosen your spine. Start with your toes and feet and work your way up your body and neck. Professional dancers do this. It's a great way to promote suppleness.
- Shake your hands and fingers for a few moments while you feel your blood flowing. Do the same with each foot.
- Alternate raising your legs to your chest. When your knee is chest-height, grab onto it, hold that position for a moment or two and then return to the starting position.
- While standing, raise yourself up on your toes, pause, return to the starting position and repeat. This will strengthen your toes and ankles.
- You'll find additional ways to exercise in the following pages.

*Chapter 10 — Stretches and Exercises for Mobility, Strength and Health*

After you have done the warm-ups listed on the prior page, start with your neck. You should practice extreme caution when exercising your neck, so do everything slowly and carefully. All of the photos on this page illustrate some of the neck exercises you can do.

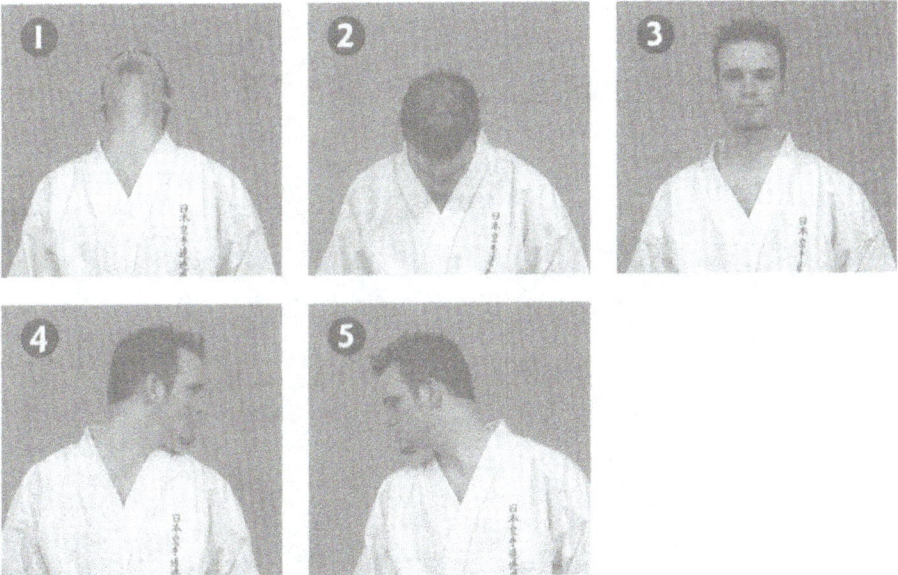

**1, 2, 3** First, you can do the up and down movements. Tilt your head back as if you were trying to touch your head to your back, then bring your neck forward until your chin touches your chest. Do this slowly, carefully and frequently.

**4, 5** Next up is the side-to-side drill. When you do this one, look over each shoulder as if you are trying to look at someone behind you. As before, repeat this exercise slowly, carefully and frequently.

Now it's time for the circular motions. Turn your head in circles, big round circles. Go to the left and to the right with these large, exaggerated moves.

*Japanese Karate: A Warrior's Spirit*

These next drills will loosen your spine and upper body, both of which are important in karate and other physical activity Even if you are not on an exercise program, it's important to stretch your spine and upper body

**1, 2, 3** When you do this drill, you can hold your hands as shown or hold your arms straight out. It's your call. Regardless of your hand position, you will turn your body from side to side as if you were trying to look behind yourself. In addition, you may also revolve your upper body/torso in large circular moves, slowly and carefully.

*Chapter 10 — Stretches and Exercises for Mobility, Strength and Health*

Some of your largest and most important muscles are in your legs. You should devote a lot of attention to keeping them loose and supple. This will improve your ability to move swiftly and smoothly and greatly aid your kicks.

To begin, bend at the waist and touch your toes. Eventually, you should be able to touch your fingertips to the ground. The large ligaments in your legs need to be loosened and stretched, but this must be done slowly and may take considerable time. If you find that you are unable to touch the ground, this only means that the process of stretching out will take some time. Do not rush it or you will risk injuring yourself.

**1, 2, 3** As you can see, you can also stretch your legs from a seated position. Try to grab your toes. When you can do that, pull your upper body down to rest on your legs.

Many of your leg stretches will be done while sitting. In the illustrations below, the black belt has easily touched his head to the ground with his legs spread as wide as possible.

*1, 2, 3, 4* Beginners should spread your legs as far as possible. If you can't stretch them as far as the next guy, don't worry. Eventually, you'll get there, too. From here, little by little, try to touch your chest toward the floor. When you're done, lower your head to one leg and then the other.

*TIP: Think of this as touching the floor with your chest rather than your head. This will help you to keep your back a bit straighter and make for a better stretch.*

*Chapter 10 — Stretches and Exercises for Mobility, Strength and Health*

**1, 2, 3** This stretch requires you to fold one leg behind you. If you are stiff, this may be difficult. If so, devote some time to resolving this problem first. If the stress is too much on your ankle, knee or hip, proceed with extreme caution. In fact, some students may not even be able to get into this position. For those of you who can, follow the illustrations of the black belt. Notice how he turns his upper body in both directions, bending his body and his leg, etc.

**4, 5, 6** The same positions seen from a different angle.

*1 and 2* In this example, fold your legs as shown. If possible, touch your feet together. Some beginners may not be able to place their knees on the ground. If that is the case for you, place a hand or elbow on each knee and slowly press downward. This is a difficult stretch, so don't force it. Do as much as possible and gradually you will improve.

For those of you who have that suppleness, you should bend your upper body to the ground.

*TIP: On all leg stretches, use extreme caution and do not force any stretch. You don't want to injure yourself*

Regardless of your age, strength exercises can help you become a better martial artist. In addition to improving your overall skills, strength exercises will reduce the likelihood of injuries. Remember, weight training is good, provided you maintain the suppleness needed for speed and agility. Therefore, strive for long, elongated muscle development. Don't neglect that stretching.

Following are some exercises that you should work into your routine.

## Sit-Ups

Sit-ups are one of the exercises you can do. Sit on the floor with your legs straight out in front of you, lay back, clasp your hands behind your head, slowly sit up and touch your elbows to your raised legs. As you are sitting up, bring both knees toward your chest. These are also called crunches.

## Leg Raises

You can also do leg raises. While sitting on the floor, straighten your legs out in front of you. Brace yourself on your forearms, raise your legs slightly, hold them for 10 seconds, raise them again, hold that position, lower them to the ground and repeat. As your abdominals gets stronger, you can hold your legs off the ground for longer periods of time.

## Light Iron

For additional strength exercises, you can also work with light weights. You can throw punches while holding weights and practice your blocks.

Normally, the legs should be strong enough without any weight training. However, you can always throw on a pair of light weights on your ankles and throw some kicks.

## Push-Ups

There are many types of push-ups you can do, including knuckle push-ups (A), push-ups on two knuckles (B), fingertip push-ups (C) and push-ups on the back of your hands (D).

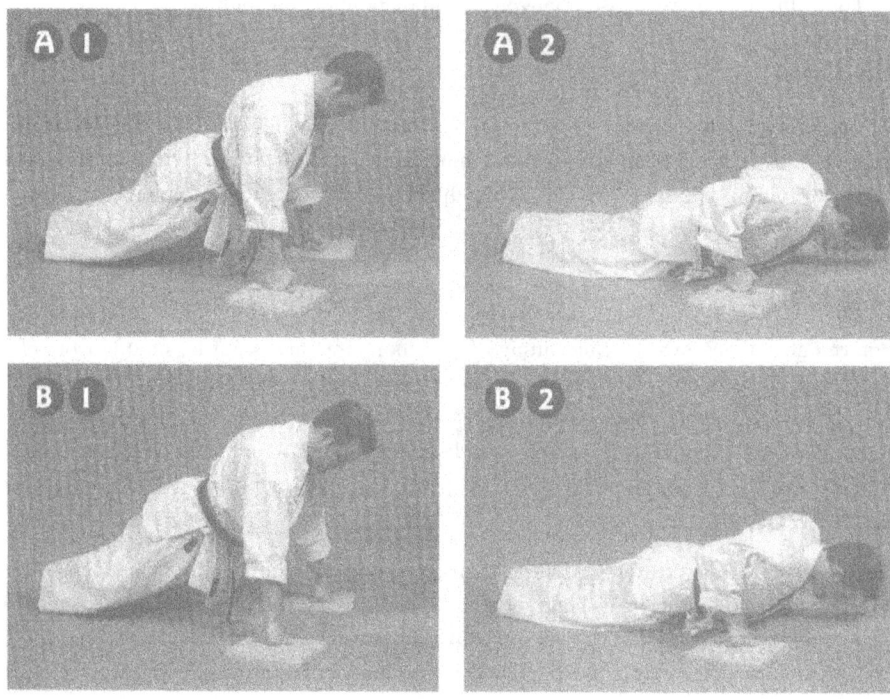

*Chapter 10 — Stretches and Exercises for Mobility, Strength and Health*

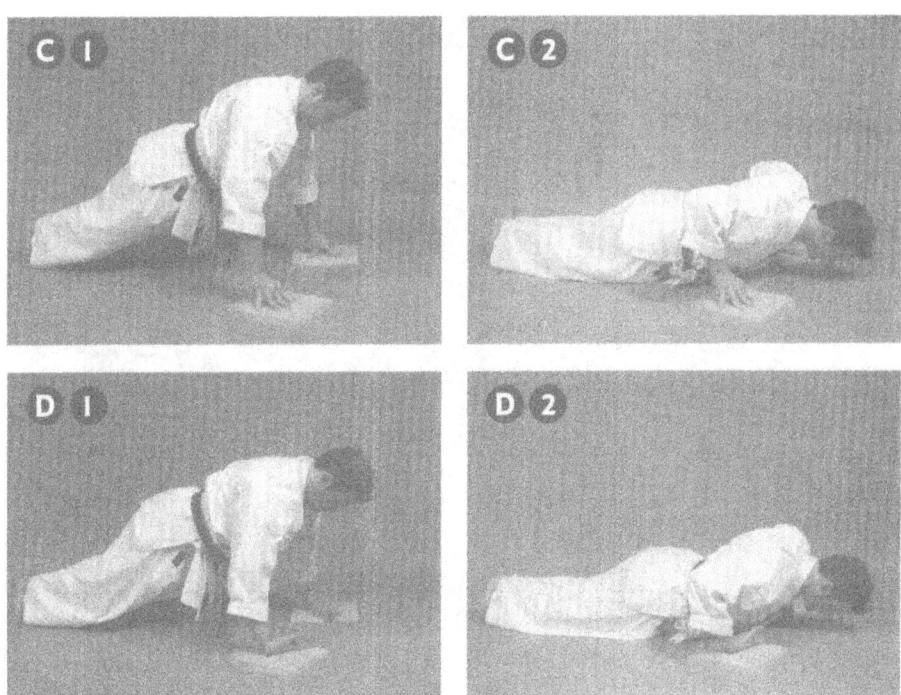

## Chapter 11

# *First Strike Concepts*

### Take the Initiative
Sen No Sen

### Respond to Attack
Go No Sen

To strike first, you must be absolutely sure you are in eminent danger from an attack. Do not place yourself in the position of being the attacker, which is a violation of the law.

In street altercations, the first strike — if delivered properly — may be all that is needed. If you stun or disable your opponent and he is not able to continue his attack, the prudent thing to do is leave the scene before the altercation escalates. Get out of there immediately.

If you seriously injure your attacker, under certain circumstances, you may wish to render aid or summon help for the injured.

And remember, according to the law, once you have defended yourself and stopped an attacker, you no longer have the right to mete out further punishment. Do not continue to strike or kick an attacker — out of anger or frustration — or you will be considered the attacker.

It's a good time to remind you again of two vital concepts to apply when practicing or defending yourself with karate:
- To achieve the utmost power, throw your techniques with kime, which is the focus of your mind and body.
- Make sure you *kiai*, which is the expelling of breath with sound. This will not only tighten your muscles, it will also unnerve an attacker, causing him to gasp or draw air into his lungs. At that moment, he will be at his weakest.

Considering all of the circumstances that justify striking first, here are some illustrations of effective techniques to practice. Apply everything from a natural stance.

1, 2, 3 These three photos illustrate an attacker and defender in a natural stance.

*Chapter 11 — First Strike Concepts*

1 A quick front kick is a good equalizer.

2 If you throw a head butt, aim for the attacker's nose, eyes or cheeks. If you go head to head, you may find that your attacker has a harder head.

3 A straight arm drive under the chin or nose can be particularly effective. A shot to the nose is more dangerous.

4 A forefinger knuckle to the attacker's throat is also a good technique. It doesn't require any strength, and it is very effective.

*1* A "claw" or throat grasp (and squeeze) cuts off the air and is quite dangerous.

*2* If you "claw" an attacker's eyes, apply only enough pressure to obscure his vision. If you apply this too hard, you will cause severe damage.

*3* A stomp to an attacker's ankle or instep works, too.

*4* Dan Ivan demonstrates a side kick to the knee or the side of the knee. You could also use a front kick.

*Chapter 11 — First Strike Concepts*

1 A backfist can be thrown to the temple, nose and other areas of the body, including the groin.

2 The backhand chop can be thrown to vulnerable targets, such as the throat, nose, etc.

3 For a rear attack, use your elbow.

4 A back headbutt can be thrown to the face.

**161**

*1* Snap upward when you throw a back heel kick.

*2* You can throw a back hook kick with your heel to the attacker's kidney or knee.

*3* A knee to the groin is always quick and effective.

"MOVING
FORWARD WITH
CONFIDENCE"

*Tanaka Hiroshi*

# Chapter 12

# Key Points and Strategies

Avoid risky areas. Remote and dark parking lots invite robbers. Some areas of cities are known for gang activities and other dangers. Avoid these areas. Isolated areas such as parks can also pose a risk. If you must travel or do business late at night, use caution. With a little planning, you may be able to change your routines or lifestyle. It's also not a bad idea to watch your attitude, too. You may have to change that to avoid an attack.

Road rage is becoming more frequent. Stay out of that mess. Plan how you would avoid this situation should it happen to you.

Don't let pride get you into a fight. If possible, walk away. It's not important whether you can win or lose. Even a "victory" may still involve police, lawsuits and other discomfort.

Seek help when faced with danger. By involving others, the attacker may reconsider his assault and leave.

If others do not wish to involve themselves and you need help desperately, try throwing an object at passing cars or through windows of homes or business. Keep in mind that serious attacks — such as rapes, assaults, robberies and even murder — go unreported because people hesitate to get involved. Someone needs to call 911.

In training, practice everything you have learned from natural positions. For example, when you're attacked, you may be standing with your arms crossed, your hands in your pockets, holding packages, etc. Therefore, you should learn

all of your strikes, kicks and blocks from different natural positions.
- Train with different footwear and in different environmental conditions, such as on pavement, grass and rain. Learn to respond while strolling, seated or even jogging.
- If available, throw objects at your assailant. To distract him, throw groceries, a handbag, a chair, etc. Defend yourself with whatever you can find. Things like a pen, stone, brick or stick. Even your belt buckle can damage an attacker. Women can use their high heel shoes. If they remove them, this will enable them to move faster and provide an object to strike an opponent with. Tools you carry in your vehicle can also be can be used. However, be absolutely sure you are justified in whatever measure you use.
- When possible, travel in groups or with a partner. When alone, walk with confidence and briskly to your destination. Always lock your car door when you are inside.

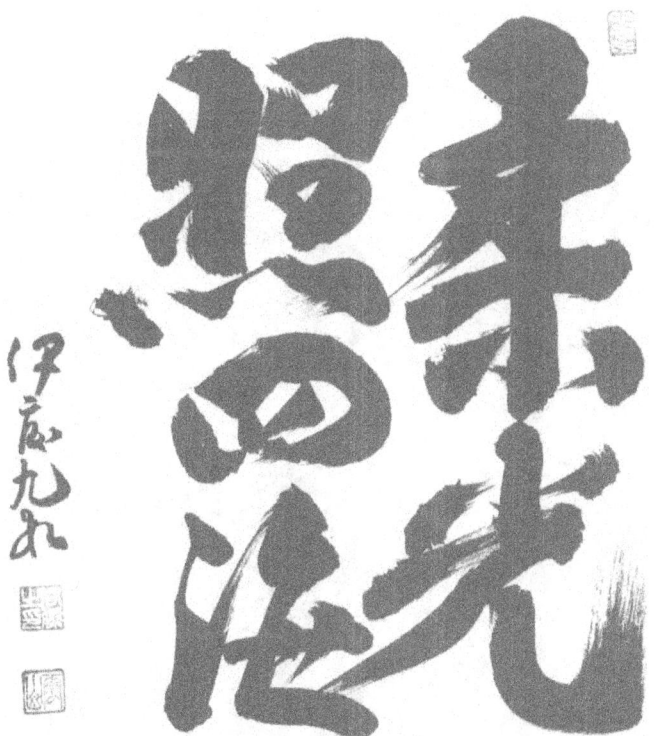

*"SOFT LIGHT ON THE FOUR SEAS"*

*Ito Kazuo, Kodokan 9th Dan*

**Chapter 13**

*Basic Terminology*

| | |
|---|---|
| **Age Uke** | Up Block |
| **Arigato** | Thank You |
| **Ate Waza** | Striking Technique |
| **Chudan** | Middle Level (solar plexus) |
| **Chudan Soto Uke** | Outside Forearm Block |
| **Chudan Uchi Uke** | Inside Forearm Block |
| **Dojo** | Training Hall |
| **Empi Uchi** | Elbow Strike |
| **Fudo** or **Sochin Dachi** | Rooted Stance |
| **Gedan** | Lower Level (below waist) |
| **Gedan Barai** | Down Block |
| **Geri Waza** | Kicking Technique |
| **Gi** | Uniform |
| **Gyaku Zuki** | Reverse Punch |
| **Hachiji Dachi** | Open Stance (ready position) |
| **Hai** | Yes |
| **Haito Uchi** | Ridgehand Strike |
| **Hangetsu Dachi** | Half-Moon Stance |

| | |
|---|---|
| **Heisoku Dachi** | Attention (feet and toes together) |
| **Hidari** | Left |
| **Ibuki** | Breathing Technique |
| **Ippon Kumite** | One-Point Sparring |
| **Jiyu Kumite** | Free-Sparring |
| **Jodan** | Upper Level (face) |
| **Juji Uke** | X Block |
| **Karate-Do** | Way of Karate |
| **Kata** | Form (example: heian shodan) |
| **Kiai** | To Yell |
| **Kiba Dachi** | Horse Stance (toes angled inward and knees bowed out over the toes |
| **Kime** | Focus of power by tensing all the muscles of the body at the moment of impact |
| **Kohai** | Junior Student |
| **Kokutsu Dachi** | Back Stance |
| **Kyotsuke** | Attention |

| | |
|---|---|
| **Ma'ai** | The correct distance of your body in relation to opponent's body and movement |
| **Migi** | Right |
| **Mokuso** | Meditate |
| **Morote Uke** | Augmented Block |
| **Musubi Dachi** | Attention (heels together, toes 45 degrees) |
| **Neko Ashi Dachi** | Cat Stance |
| **Nukite Uchi** | Spearhand Strike |
| **Obi** | Belt |
| **Oitsuki** | Lunge Punch |
| **Onegaishimasu** | Please |
| **Osae Uke** | Pressing Block |
| **Otoshi Uke** | Dropping Block (jion) |
| **Rei** | Bow |
| **Sagiashi Dachi** | Crane Stance |
| **Sanbon Kumite** | Three-Point Sparring |
| **Sanchin Dachi** | Hourglass Stance |

Chapter 13 — Basic Terminology

| | |
|---|---|
| **Seiza** | Sit |
| **Sempai** | Senior Students |
| **Sensei** | Instructor |
| **Shiko Dachi** | Square Stance (toes angled out at 45 degrees) |
| **Shuto Uke** | Knife-Hand Block |
| **Teisho Uchi** | Palm Heel Strike |
| **Tetsui Uchi** | Hammer Fist Strike |
| **Tsuki** | Punch |
| **Uke** | Block |
| **Uraken Uchi** | Backfist Strike |
| **Yame** | Stop |
| **Yoi** | Ready Position |
| **Zenkutsu Dachi** | Forward Stance |

**173**

www.ingramcontent.com/pod-product-compliance
Lightning Source LLC
Chambersburg PA
CBHW070943230426
43666CB00011B/2548